Revealing Educational Philosophy of M.K. Ghandhi and it's Relevance in Today's Scenario

by

Firdous Ahamd Malik
Shubeena Salaam
Altaf Ahmad Sheikh

Double9 BOOKS

Revealing Educational Philosophy of M.K Ghandhi and it's Relevance in Today's Scenario

by Firdous Ahamd Malik, Shubeena Salaam, Altaf Ahmad Sheikh

ISBN: 978-93-62764-24-9

Published by

DOUBLE 9 BOOKS

2/13-B, Ansari Road
Daryaganj, New Delhi – 110002
info@double9books.com
www.double9books.com
Tel. 011-40042856

ABOUT THE AUTHOR

Mr. Firdous Ahmad Malik was born at Malikpora Pulwama. He has completed his masters in Political Science from Islamic University of Science and Technology (IUST). He is currently pursuing his Masters in Education (M.ED) at the University of Kashmir. Mr. Firdous has also done a Masters in Islamic Studies as well as a Bachelor of Education (B.ED.). Heis a vivid writer and has already authored his debut book "Indo- Pak Bi-Lateral Relations: Nature of conflicts and Remedies for Peace Process". Besides, he has published a few research papers in national and international journals.

Miss. Shubeena salaam pursued her Bachelor of Arts (B.A.), Bachelor of Education (B.ED.) and a Masters in History from Kashmir University. She is currently pursuing her Masters in Education (M.ED.) at the University of Kashmir. She has attended a number of seminars, conferences and workshops related to her subject.

Mr. Altaf Ahmad Sheikh was born at Sugain Khag Budgam. He has completed his master's in sociology. In addition, Mr. Altaf has also done a Bachelor of Education (B.ED) and Masters of Education (M.ED). Mr Altaf has presented many lectures in the MOOCS programme. The author has participated in several workshops, conferences, and seminars related to his subject. He has presented different papers in different national and international seminars. He has also done NET and JRF in education. Besides, he has published a few research papers and book chapters in national journals. He is currently pursuing his integrated M.Phil /Ph.D (2024) in education at the University of Kashmir.

CONTENTS

Dedicated

To
Our teachers and parents

PREFACE

Mahatma Gandhi's values and his vision of what constituted a truly civilized and free India; it was not surprising that he developed firm views on education. Education not only molds the new generation, but reflects a society's fundamental assumptions about itself and the individuals which compose it. His experience in South Africa not only changed his outlook on politics but also helped him to see the role education played in that struggle. He was aware that he had been a beneficiary of western education and for a number of years while he was in South Africa he still tried to persuade Indians to take advantage of it. However, it was not until the early years of this century, when he was in his middle thirties, that he became so opposed to English education that he could write about ' the rottenness of this education' and that ' to give millions a knowledge of English is to enslave them... that, by receiving English education, we have enslaved the nation.' He was enraged that he had to speak of Home Rule or independence in what was clearly a foreign tongue that he could not Patrice in court in his mother tongue that all official documents were in English as were all the best newspapers and that education was carried out in English for the chosen few. He did not blame the colonial powers for this. He saw that it was quite logical that they would want elite of native Indians to become like their rulers in both manners and values. In this way, the empire could be consolidated. Gandhi blamed his fellow Indians for accepting the situation. Later in his life he was to declare that 'real freedom will come only when we free ourselves of the domination of western education, western culture and western way of living which have been ingrained in us... Emancipation from this culture would mean real freedom for us'.

As we have seen, Gandhi had not only rejected colonial education but also put forward a radical alternative. So what was this alternative? What was so radical about it? Gandhi's proposal intended to stand the education system on its head. The social philosophy and the curriculum of what he called 'basic education' thus favored the child belonging to the lowest stratum of society in such a way it implied a programme of social transformation. It sought to alter the symbolic meaning of 'education' and to change the established structure of opportunities for education.

The text presents Gandian educational thought in pros and cons. certainly, this book will help the readers to systematize their ideas about Gandhi's educational thought and provide them the glimpse of the original ideas and thinking about various aspects of education, which are definitely products of his creative genius.

This book has been thoroughly prepared and brought up-to-date to meet the requirements of readers especially M.A Education & M.ED Programme according to the revised and updated M.A and M.ED programme and also covers undergraduate syllabi of Indian Universities. Planned as a text book for students, it can also serve as a handy reference manual for practicing teachers and scholars in Gandian educational philosophy. The subject matters have been presented in a simple but in an intelligent manner and language used is simple and lucid.

Firdous Ahamd Malik,

Shubeena Salaam and

Altaf Ahmad Sheikh

(Research Scholar, University of Kashmir)

ACKNOWLEDGEMENT

All Praises to almighty Allah, the most Gracious, Beneficent and Merciful for bestowing us Courage, patience, persistence, strength and the opportunity to complete this work.

It is our privilege to express respectful feeling and gratitude to our esteemed, inspiring and meritorious teacher's especially Dr. Shabnum Qureshi, Dr. Sabahat Aslam and Miss Aafiya Hamid (full-time researcher at education department, Kashmir University) for their creative guidance, constant encouragement, sound criticism and insistence on better quality. I have no words to express gratitude to them.

Moreover, we wish to acknowledge and give thanks to the staff members of Members of (IUST Library, central library kashmir University, department library of education department of kashmir university, SPS Library Srinagar, District Library of Pulwama and Budgam) for their kind support and sympathetic attitude for making us available books, and other material required to complete this book.

We wish to acknowledge the support we received from our education department of university of Kashmir and moral support from our teachers and colleagues during the preparation of this work. We thank our academic fraternity, who has made valuable suggestions after reading through the various parts of the manuscript. We also wish to thank the anonymous referees for their constructive criticism and suggestions, which have helped us in improving the work.

This book would not have possible without the extraordinary support of our family members, relatives and friends especially Miss Bisma, thank you all for being a part of our life.

We thank you readers; you are the best judge and our source o f inspiration. Without your support it would not have been possible for us to keep on writing. Please write/mail your views and valuable suggestions for improvement of this book. Happy Reading!!!

Firdous Ahmad Malik

Shubeena Salam and Altaf Ahmad Sheikh

Email- Shaheenfirdous123@gmail.com saltafsedu@gmail.com

TIME LINE OF SIGNIFICANT EVENTS IN THE LIFE OF MAHATMA GANDHI

1869	Born on 02nd October
1893	Faced racial discrimination in South Africa
1894	Founded the 'Natal Indian congress.
1904	Established 'Phoenix settlement'.
1910	Established Tolstoy Fram
1915	Joined the Indian National Congress
1918	First Hunger Strike at kheda, Gujrat
1919	Launched Non-cooperation movement (NCM)
1922	Policeman at Chauri Chaura Killed.
1924	Presided over the Belgaum Congress.
1930	Leads the Salt March (Dandi March)
1931	Gandhi- Irwin Pact signed
1932	Civil disobedience movement
1932	Poona Pact Signed.
1932	'Harijan Sevak Sangh' established.
1934	Resigned from the congress
1939	Wrote a letter to Adolf Hitler
1942	Launched ' Quite India' movement
1948	Assassinated by Nathuram Godse in New Delhi.
1948	Cremated on the banks of the river Yamuna by Ramdas.
2007	UNGA declared October 2 as international Day of Non-violence.

Chapter 1
Life, Upbringing and Education

LIFE AND UPBRINGING

Mohandas Karamchand Gandhi was the preeminent leader of the Indian independence movement in British-ruled India. Mohandas Karamchand Gandhi was born on 2 October 1869 to a Hindu Modh Baniya family in Porbandar (also known as *Sudamapuri*), a coastal town on the Kathiawar Peninsula and then part of the small princely state of Porbandar in the Kathiawar Agency of the Indian Empire. His full name was Mohandas Karamchand Gandhi, but for corers of people, he was a "Bapu" or the father of Nation or Rashtrapita. His first name was Mohan which was the name of Lord Shri Krishna who is called Jagadgura or Yogiaancha Yogi or a "Stitpradnya". Employing nonviolent civil disobedience, Gandhi led India to independence and inspired movements for civil rights and freedom across the world.

Gandhi loved his country, people, and culture, took pride in them. He was a nationalist bounded by universalism; but if choice has to be made between India and Truth, he said, he would be for Truth. He taught us a national self-respect and freed us from the intellectual bondage of the west. He inspired us with his new dreams visions, and revolutionized our ways of living and thinking. The love and service of his people was his Dream.

Gandhi had many friends from abroad. One of them was Romain Rolland. Rolland and Gandhi had a very delightful and non-conventional relationship. Romain Rolland (RR) was older by four years than Gandhi, and yet he put Gandhi at father's level. RR put himself in position as a son and a disciple. He used to refer to Gandhi as "Our master", "the holiness of the master", and the "Guru". RR used to say that Gandhi was better than himself, that he was normally inferior to Gandhi. He had a very fascinating and complex relationship with the masses that venerated and worshipped him as a God. This was so not because of any promises or any demagogic tricks or misleading "oratory". The relationship between Gandhi and intellectuals was, however not always pleasant.

Gandhi's deepest strivings were spiritual. He said he did not know any religion other than the religion of activity and more activity. Although the whole world addresses him as "Bapu" and "Father of Nation", it is to remembered that he possessed capacity to shower material love, and he had passion for nursing the sick, he was called by some persons as " Bapu my mother".

Gandhiji had a knack of achieving results of Himalayan proportions from apparently small things. He was the earliest visionary of "Small is beautiful". It is recognized, accepted that he was one of the first leaders who raised the alarm about environmental destruction and ecological decay. Let us note three episodes in his life which prove this point.

First, to begin with, he did not mind accepting flowers whenever they were given to him as a mark of welcome. Soon he realized that by accepting flowers at meetings (which were many) he was contributing to environmental destruction. Therefore, at some stage he stopped accepting flowers, and asked people to welcome him by giving yarn spinned by the hosts.

Second instance occurred in his Ashram. A tender branch or twig of a Neem tree or Babul tree was his tooth brush obtained fresh every day from the surroundings. One day, an Ashramite was asked by Gandhiji to get him the tooth brush he needed. After a while, that person presented himself before Gandhiji with a fairly big branch of Neem tree. Gandhiji was surprised and irritated by this, and asked the said person why he brought such a big branch when only a tiny one was needed. The person said that there are so many Neem trees in the Ashram premises, and why one should object if somewhat big branch was cut for Bapu's needs. Gandhiji made him understand that only one Gandhi is not the user of Neem branches, there are many such users. If we cut such big branches for everyone, soon we would make this earth treeless which is a great threat to the survival of our planet.

The third episode is so awesome, and it makes one feel that Gandhiji would always remain an enigma to us. Gandhiji had spent some time experimenting to find out what is the optimum quantity of water an average person would require to be cleaned after going to toilet. It would be instructive to search for result he had got from archives.

Through his various experiments, his capacity to love expanded, and by the end of his life he was aflame with love. He had insatiable love for mankind. Wonder struck with the heights of his achievements, the people would ask him the secret of his success, the secret of his life. He would tell them in the simplest of words the profoundest truths. Asked for a message, he replied, *'my life is my message.'* Asked for his secret of life, he replied, *'Renounce and enjoy.'*

The speech he gave before the House of Commons when he went to England to participate in Round Table Conference, was so compelling and impressive that a few members of audience asked Mahadeva Desai, Gandhis Secretary, as to how Gandhi is able to speak so well for such a long time without ant preparation, without any promptings, without any notes? Mahadev Desai has said, Gandhi is an effective speaker because what he thinks, what he feels, what he says, and what he does are all one.

It has been said that Gandhiji personality was full of grandeur or magnificence. He was a great apostle of non-violence and revolution; he was a revolutionary par excellence. He advocated decentralization; small is beautiful, arcadian civilization, *Sarvodaya samuhik* inspiration. The story of life of Gandhiji was heroic; there was a genuine, real, honest transformation from Mohan to Mahatma. But Mahatma shared the destiny of *Maharshi Vyas* towards the end of his life. The pathos of this disillusionment has been lost on people.

Gandhi had "Sakshatkar" of Gita's *"karmayoga"*, and there was unity in internal and external of his beings. Gita's *"Stitpradnya"* is personified in Gandhi. Gandhi-the *"Stitpradnya"* Compassionate, affectionate great man *(Mahapurush)* – Satpurush, Social scientist of the order of writers of smritis, exceptionally great man *(nirala Mahapurush)*, in lighter vein, one may say that English dictionary would be inadequate to describe Gandhi. We, however, may choose a thousand names and make "Gandhi Sahastranam" as a substitute.

Gandhi gave to his family the nature of Ashramas. Further, his ideas targeted to make *Grihastashram* into *Sanyasashram* without requiring him or without adopting the attire of the Sanyasin. Both Gandhi had a phenomenal energy which they utilized for working on diverse activities. Their humility, fearlessness, Sense of humor, faith in prayer was of high order. Both were the seekers, experimenters in Truth and Ashram. Their most important experiments were not in mundane matters; they were in the art of living, how to live meaningfully in the world that is full of violence, conflicts, incessant change.

Gandhiji was called *Nanga Fakir* (naked saint) by Winston Churchill. He was ignorant about the rich traditions in India. Otherwise, he would not have used such words.

Gandhiji school career was a failure. He wanted to be a doctor but could not become one because of failure. Gandhi become a strong votary or advocate of simplicity of life and minimization of wants, the importance, the value, the necessity of which he was, in a way, forced to learn when he was in England as a student and was enamored by gentlemanly life style for a while. The period proved to be highly formative because he instilled in himself the values of self-reliance, frugality, physical endurance. One of the great points of Gandhi's strength was his being impervious to ridicule, scorn, etc.

It has been said that services and suffering wanted to take a human form and Gandhi was born. *Bhagavad Gita* was the "Spiritual Reference book" for Gandhi.

About his own non-violence, Gandhiji has made a very strong claim that he has become incapable of hating any being on our planet. He has said, 'by a long course of prayerful discipline, I have ceased for over 40 years to hate anybody. I make this point in all humility. My non-cooperation has its root in love and not in hatred'.

Gandhiji explains further the nature of Non-violence by saying that Satyagraha is gentle; it must not be the result of anger or malice. It is never impatient, vociferous, and it was conceived as a complete substitute for violence.

Gandhiji used to say. 'We must hate the sin, the evil, not the sinner, evil-doer'. Non-violence is an extremely active force; it has no room for cowardice or even weaknesses. The strength does not come from physical capacity. It comes from an indomitable will. Gandhi can be given as the best examples of this formulation.

Gandhiji used to say "my life is an indivisible whole, and all of my activities run into one another, and their origin is in insatiable love for mankind".

The eternal Christ-like humility made Gandhi to make profound statements such as the follows:

'I have nothing new to teach the world. Truth and non-violence are as old as the hills.... My philosophy, if it may be called by that pretentions name, is contained in what I have said. But you will not call it "Gandhism" I have held faster than ever to the position that truth may not be sacrificed for anything whatsoever. Those who believe in the simple truth I have laid down can propagate them only by living them.'

It is but natural that Gandhi should have been influenced by many persons, and Gandhi has acknowledged this influence. It is remarkable that he has frankly and lovingly and honestly acknowledged the influence

Kasturba, his wife, has exerted him. He said that he learnt the theory and method of Satyagraha from her. He has said that he learnt the lesson of non-violence from his wife. "When I tried to bend her to my will, because of her determination to resist, and to ready for suffering, ultimately made me ashamed of myself.'

Gandhi has been persistently criticized by many that his ideas, methods, programmes were impracticable or utopian, unrealistic. He used to reject this charge saying that he had not the shadow of doubt that any man can achieve what he had achieved if he works and makes the same effort and cultivate the same hope and faith. We can liken this assurance to the assurance given by Krishna in Gita. To recall, Krishna had promised the following:

Yada yada hi dharmasya glanirbhavati Bharats
Abhyut hanamd harmasya tadatmanam srujamyaham.

Gandhi has revived the typical Indian tradition of establishing "Ashramas", but while doing so he transformed the tradition by giving it new meaning, new scope. Family became an Ashram and Ashram became a family under his leadership. Without wearing the attire of "Sanyasi" (monk, who has embraced the life of complete renunciation), he transformed "Grihastashram" into "Sanyasashram". It was his aim, his plan that every village should have an "Ashrama". Gandhi has been revered, worshipped, and reviled. The range of epithets showered on him has been mind-bogglingly wide indeed-stage, saint, genius, crank, and faddist and so on. He was called Christ, Buddha, Mahavir, and Nanak and so on. There has not been any great man whose name has not been given to him.

It was Gandhi originality and intuition that he added completely new things to "Ashram System". He made it flexible. He emphasized greatly the importance of and need for "Brahmacharya". He put forth the idea (and practiced it) that "Brahmacharya" can be and should be practiced in "Grihastashram" also. Gandhi's high discernment is reflected in his view that what is applicable, what is relevant to the individual is true for the society, collectively also.

It is known to many that one of the Gandhis traits was to immediately put into practice what one comes to be believed in. Gandhi was not any one individual; he had become the pulse, feeling of the entire nation.

Gandhi famously led Indians in challenging the British-imposed salt tax with the 400 km (250 mi) Dandi Salt March in 1930, and later in calling for the British to *Quit India* in 1942. He was imprisoned for many years, upon many occasions, in both South Africa and India. One of Gandhi's major strategies, first in South Africa and then in India, was uniting Muslims and Hindus to work together in opposition to British imperialism. In 1919–22 he won strong Muslim support for his leadership in the Khilafat Movement to support the historic Ottoman Caliphate. By 1924, that Muslim support had largely evaporated.

Time magazine named Gandhi the Man of the Year in 1930. Gandhi was also the runner-up to Albert Einstein as "Person of the Century" at the end of 1999. The Government of India awarded the annual Gandhi Peace Prize to distinguished social workers, world leaders and citizens. Nelson Mandela, the leader of South Africa's struggle to eradicate racial discrimination and segregation, was a prominent non-Indian recipient. In 2011, *Time* magazine named Gandhi as one of the top 25 political icons of all time. Gandhi did not receive the Nobel Peace Prize, although he was nominated five times between 1937 and 1948, including the first-ever nomination by the American Friends Service Committee, though he made the short list only twice, in 1937 and 1947.

Indians widely describe Gandhi as the father of the nation. In 2007, the United Nations General Assembly declared Gandhi's birthday 2 October as "the International Day of Nonviolence.

Education

When Gandhi was 9 years old he went to a local school at Rajkot and studied the basics of arithmetic, history, geography, and languages. At the age of 11, he went to a high school in Rajkot. Because of his wedding, at least about one year, his studies were disturbed and later he joined and completed his schooling. He joined Samaldas College in Bhavnagar in 1888 at Gujarat. Later, one of his family friends Mavji Dave Joshi pursued further studies i.e. law in London. Gandhiji was not satisfied with his studies at Samaldas College and so he became excited by the London proposal and managed to convince his mother and wife that he will not touch non-veg, wine, or women.

"First they ignore you, then they laugh at you, then they fight with you, then you win." - Mahatma Gandhi

Off to London

In the year 1888, Mahatma Gandhi left for London to study law. Thereafter 10 days after arrival, he joined the Inner Temple, one of the four London law colleges, and studied and practiced law. In London, he also joined a Vegetarian Society and was introduced to Bhagavad Gita by some of his vegetarian friends. Later, Bhagavad Gita set an impression and influenced his life.

WORKS AUTHORED BY MAHAMATA GHANDI

Important publications on education and having bearing on education are:

1. My experiments with truth. (Autobiography)
2. Basic Education
3. Towards need education
4. True Education
5. To the students
6. Task before Indian Student
7. India of My dreams
8. Medium off Instruction
9. Tasks before India

Gandhiji also wrote extensively on education in *Harijan*—a paper founded by him.

LIFE IN SOUTH AFRICA

At 23, Gandhi again left his family and set off for the British-governed Natal province in South Africa in May 1893. After a week, Gandhi was asked to go to the Dutch-governed Transvaal province. When Gandhi boarded the train, railroad officials ordered him to move to the third-class car. Gandhi, holding first-class tickets, refused. A policeman threw him off the train.

As Gandhi talked to Indians in South Africa, he learned that such experiences were common. Sitting in the cold depot that first night of his trip, Gandhi debated returning to India or fighting the discrimination. He decided that he couldn't ignore these injustices.

Gandhi spent 20 years bettering Indians' rights in South Africa, becoming a resilient, potent leader against discrimination. He learned about Indian grievances, studied the law, wrote letters to officials, and organized petitions. On May 22, 1894, Gandhi established the Natal Indian Congress (NIC). Although it began as an organization for wealthy Indians, Gandhi expanded it to all classes and castes. He became a leader of South Africa's Indian community, his activism covered by newspapers in England and India.

RETURN TO INDIA

In 1896 after three years in South Africa, Gandhi sailed to India to bring his wife and two sons back with him, returning in November. Gandhi's ship was quarantined at the harbor for 23 days, but the real reason for the delay was an angry mob of whites at the dock who believed Gandhi was returning with Indians who would overrun South Africa.

Gandhi sent his family to safety, but he was assaulted with bricks, rotten eggs, and fists. Police escorted him away. Gandhi refuted the claims against him but refused to prosecute those involved. The violence stopped, strengthening Gandhi's prestige.

Influenced by the "Gita," Gandhi wanted to purify his life by following the concepts of aparigraha (nonpossession) and samabhava (equitability). A friend gave him "Unto This Last" by John Ruskin, which inspired Gandhi to establish Phoenix Settlement, a community outside Durban, in June 1904. The settlement focused on eliminating needless possessions and living in full equality. Gandhi moved his family and his newspaper, the Indian Opinion, to the settlement.

In 1906, believing that family life was detracting from his potential as a public advocate; Gandhi took the vow of *brahmacharya* (abstinence from sex). He simplified his vegetarianism to unspiced, usually uncooked foods—mostly fruits and nuts, which he believed would help quiet his urges.

SATYAGRAHA

Gandhi believed that his vow of *brahmacharya* allowed him the focus to devise the concept of *Satyagraha* in late 1906. In the simplest sense, *Satyagraha* is passive resistance, but Gandhi described it as "truth force,"or natural right. He believed exploitation was possible only if the exploited and the exploiter accepted it, so seeing beyond the current situation provided power to change it.

In practice, *Satyagraha* is nonviolent resistance to injustice. A person using *Satyagraha* could resist injustice by refusing to follow an unjust law or putting up with physical assaults and/or confiscation of his property without anger. There would be no winners or losers; all would understand the "truth" and agree to rescind the unjust law.

Gandhi first organized *Satyagraha* against the Asiatic Registration Law, or Black Act, which passed in March 1907. It required all Indians to be fingerprinted and carry registration documents at all times. Indians refused fingerprinting and picketed documentation offices. Protests were organized, miners went on strike, and Indians illegally traveled from Natal to the Transvaal in opposition to the act. Many protesters, including Gandhi, were beaten and arrested. After seven years of protest, the Black Act was repealed. The nonviolent protest had succeeded.

BACK TO INDIA

After 20 years in South Africa, Gandhi returned to India. By the time he arrived, press reports of his South African triumphs had made him a national hero. He traveled the country for a year before beginning reforms. Gandhi found that his fame conflicted with observing conditions of the poor, so he wore a loincloth (*dhoti*) and sandals, the garb of the masses, during this journey. In cold weather, he added a shawl. This became his lifetime wardrobe.

Gandhi founded another communal settlement in Ahmadabad called Sabarmati Ashram. For the next 16 years, Gandhi lived there with his family.

He was also given the honorary title of Mahatma, or "Great Soul." Many credit Indian poet Rabindranath Tagore, winner of the 1913 Nobel Prize for Literature, for awarding Gandhi this name. Peasants viewed Gandhi as a holy man, but he disliked the title because it implied he was special. He viewed himself as ordinary.

After the year ended, Gandhi still felt stifled because of World War I. As part of Satyagraha, Gandhi had vowed never to take advantage of an opponent's troubles. With the British in a major conflict, Gandhi couldn't fight them for Indian freedom. Instead, he used Satyagraha to erase inequities among Indians. Gandhi persuaded landlords to stop forcing tenant farmers to pay increased rent by appealing to their morals and fasted to convince mill owners to settle a strike. Because of Gandhi's prestige, people didn't want to be responsible for his death from fasting.

CONFRONTING BRITISH

When the war ended, Gandhi focused on the fight for Indian self-rule (*Swaraj*). In 1919, the British handed Gandhi a cause: the Rowlett Act, which gave the British nearly free rein to detain "revolutionary" elements without trial. Gandhi organized a *hartal* (strike), which began on March 30, 1919. Unfortunately, the protest turned violent.

Gandhi ended the hartal once he heard about the violence, but more than 300 Indians had died and more than 1,100 were injured from British reprisals in the city of Amritsar. Satyagraha hadn't been achieved, but the

Amritsar Massacre fueled Indian opinions against the British. The violence showed Gandhi that the Indian people didn't fully believe in Satyagraha. He spent much of the 1920s advocating for it and struggling to keep protests peaceful.

Gandhi also began advocating self-reliance as a path to freedom. Since the British established India as a colony, Indians had supplied Britain with raw fiber and then imported the resulting cloth from England. Gandhi advocated that Indians spin their own cloth, popularizing the idea by traveling with a spinning wheel, often spinning yarn while giving a speech. The image of the spinning wheel (*charkha*) became a symbol for independence.

In March 1922, Gandhi was arrested and sentenced to six years in prison for sedition. After two years, he was released following surgery to find his country embroiled in violence between Muslims and Hindus. When Gandhi began a 21-day fast still ill from surgery, many thought he would die, but he rallied. The fast created a temporary peace.

SALT MARCH

In December 1928, Gandhi and the Indian National Congress (INC) announced a challenge to the British government. If India wasn't granted Commonwealth status by December 31, 1929, they would organize a nationwide protest against British taxes. The deadline passed without change.

Gandhi chose to protest the British salt tax because salt was used in everyday cooking, even by the poorest. The Salt March began a nationwide boycott starting March 12, 1930, when Gandhi and 78 followers walked 200 miles from the Sabarmati Ashram to the sea. The group grew along the way, reaching 2,000 to 3,000. When they reached the coastal town of Dandi on April 5, they prayed all night. In the morning, Gandhi made a presentation of picking up a piece of sea salt from the beach. Technically, he had broken the law.

Thus began an endeavor for Indians to make salt. Some picked up loose salt on the beaches, while others evaporated saltwater. Indian-made salt soon was sold nationwide. Peaceful picketing and marches were conducted. The British responded with mass arrests.

PROTESTERS BEATEN

When Gandhi announced a march on the government-owned Dharasana Saltworks, the British imprisoned him without trial. Although they hoped

Gandhi's arrest would stop the march, they underestimated his followers. The poet Sarojini Naidu led 2,500 marchers. As they reached the waiting police, the marchers were beaten with clubs. News of the brutal beating of peaceful protesters shocked the world.

British viceroy Lord Irwin met with Gandhi and they agreed on the Gandhi-Irwin Pact, which granted limited salt production and freedom for the protesters if Gandhi called off the protests. While many Indians believed that Gandhi hadn't gotten enough from the negotiations, he viewed it as a step toward independence.

INDEPENDENCE

After the success of the Salt March, Gandhi conducted another fast that enhanced his image as a holy man or prophet. Dismayed at the adulation, Gandhi retired from politics in 1934 at age 64. He came out of retirement five years later when the British viceroy announced, without consulting Indian leaders, that India would side with England during World War II. This revitalized the Indian independence movement.

Many British parliamentarians realized they were facing mass protests and began discussing an independent India. Although Prime Minister Winston Churchill opposed losing India as a colony, the British announced in March 1941 that it would free India after World War II. Gandhi wanted independence sooner and organized a "Quit India" campaign in 1942. The British again jailed Gandhi.

HINDU-MUSLIM CONFLICT

When Gandhi was released in 1944, independence seemed near. Huge disagreements, however, arose between Hindus and Muslims. Because the majority of Indians were Hindu, Muslims feared losing political power if India became independent. The Muslims wanted six provinces in northwest India, where Muslims predominated, to become an independent country. Gandhi opposed partitioning India and tried to bring the sides together, but that proved too difficult even for the Mahatma.

Violence erupted; entire towns were burned. Gandhi toured India, hoping his presence could curb the violence. Although violence stopped where Gandhi visited, he couldn't be everywhere.

PARTITION

The British, seeing India headed for civil war, decided to leave in August 1947. Before leaving, they got the Hindus, against Gandhi's wishes, to agree to a partition plan. On August 15, 1947, Britain granted independence to India and to the newly formed Muslim country of Pakistan.

Millions of Muslims marched from India to Pakistan, and millions of Hindus in Pakistan walked to India. Many refugees died from illness, exposure, and dehydration. As 15 million Indians became uprooted from their homes, Hindus and Muslims attacked each other.

Gandhi once again went on a fast. He would only eat again, he stated, once he saw clear plans to stop the violence. The fast began on January 13, 1948. Realizing that the frail, aged Gandhi couldn't withstand a long fast, the sides collaborated. On January 18, more than 100 representatives approached Gandhi with a promise for peace, ending his fast.

DEATH

Not everyone approved of the plan. Some radical Hindu groups believed that India shouldn't have been partitioned, blaming Gandhi. On January 30, 1948, the 78-year-old Gandhi spent his day discussing issues. Just past 5 p.m., Gandhi began the walk, supported by two grandnieces, to the Birla House, where he was staying in New Delhi, for a prayer meeting. A crowd surrounded him. A young Hindu named Nathuram Godse stopped before him and bowed. Gandhi bowed back. Godse shot Gandhi three times. Although Gandhi had survived five other assassination attempts, he fell to the ground, dead.

Chapter 2
Gandhis Nai Talim (Basic Education)
Part I

WHAT IS NAI TALIM (NT)? WHAT IT IS NOT?

Put it simply, Talim means education, training; Nai means new; together, it means new education. Nai Talim is known by some other names also. It could mean educational system which is better than the existing, prevailing educational system. Nai Talim also means Buniyadi education, Basic education, Wardha scheme, Nitya Nayi Talim (NNT); Gandhi system, National or Rashtriya education.

Nai Talim is a life philosophy; it is not the creation of merely some rigid, Straight-jacket organization or framework. It would be free, independent, autonomous institution. Nai Talim is *"Jeevan Darshanam"*. It paradigm has global/universal vision; its social organization is the aim of NT. It is radical, revolutionary system.

At Round Table Conference in London (1931) Mohandas Karamchand Gandhi, also known as Mahatma Gandhi pointed out the ineffectiveness of the primary education system of India and the low percentage of literacy rate among Indian people. He blamed the policy of the British Government responsible for the pathetic situation in the field of mass education. Gandhiji described the main defects of the system of education as, "I am fully convinced that present system of education is not only wasteful but positively harmful. They would pick up evil habits. English has created a permanent bar between the highly educated few and the uneducated many." He further said, "let us now cry a halt and concentrate on educating the child properly through manual work not as a side activity but as a prime means of intellectual activity" (Maheswari). Mahatma Gandhi proposed his scheme of Basic Education (Nai Talim) in a well formulated approach to education in 1937 in his newspaper 'Harijan'. In order to discuss different aspects of the scheme of education, an All India education conference was held in Wardha on 22nd and 23rd October, 1937. The conference is called Wardha Educational Conference and Gandhiji himself presided over the conference. After serious discussions, the following four resolutions were passed in the conference (Maheswari).

1) Free and compulsory education is to be provided for seven years on a nationwide scale.

2) Mother tongue should be the medium of instruction.

3) The process of education throughout this period should have some manual and productive work and ability should be developed to engage them with handicraft work according to the environment of the child.

4) The proposed system of education would gradually be able to generate remuneration of the teachers.

Basic education or Nai Talim was based on the fundamental principle of "learning by doing". Gandhiji believed on action and hence his concepts of basic education can be classified as activity method or practical method. It was mainly a method of co-relation between book learning and doing activity through craft like gardening, weaving, spinning, carpentry, etc. According to him, a realistic scheme of education must be closely integrated with the physical and social environment of the student (Gandhi). He said, "It is called the new method of education, for it is not a foreign importation or imposition, but is consistent with the environment in India which is predominantly made up of villages. It believes in establishing equilibrium between the body, the mind and the spirit of which man is made. It is unlike the Western type which is predominantly militarist, in which the mind and the body are the primary care of education to the subordination of the spirit. This is best done when education is given through handicrafts. The other specialty is that it is designed to be wholly self-supporting. It does not, therefore, demand an expenditure of millions on education." (Harijan, 11-5-1947, p.147)

It is necessary to understand the newness of *Nayee Taleem*. The new scheme of basic education will retain whatever was good in the old system. However, it will have newness in abundance. If there is something genuinely new in it, it should result in hope taking up place of despondency, food of poverty, work of unemployment, unity of dissensions and in our boys and girls learning along with reading and writing some craft, for only through the latter will they gain the knowledge of the alphabet. *(Utmanzai, 14 October 1938 (CW 67, P. 438))*

Factors that influenced Gandhis Philosophy of Education

Following were the chief influences which had a great effect on Gandhis philosophy of education.

1. *Mothers influence*: Gandhis mother taught him the lesson of simplicity and piety.
2. *Three great thinkers*:
   I. Rayachand Bhai Patel who taught Gandhiji the first lesson in non-violence.
   II. Ruskin, through his book *unto the last drew* his attention to the principle of dignity of lobour.
   III. Leo Tolstoy's *The Kingdom of the God is within you* greatly influenced his spiritual outlook.
3. *The phoenix Settlement* (South Africa) were Gandhiji conducted early experiments.
4. *The Tolstoy farm*: in 1911, Gandhiji started an Ashram in transwal. It was here that Gandhiji helped children in their all-round development. He taught vocations such as cooking, digging and massage work. The medium of instruction was mother-tongue. English was also taught. Children learnt by doing. Textbooks were not used. No punishment was administered. Creed of non- violence was put into partice in letter and spirit.
5. *The Sabarmati Ashram*: A school was attached with the Ashram which Gandhiji wanted to become a model school.

Development of body, mind and spirit

The English word 'education' etymologically means 'drawing out'. That means an Endeavour to develop our latent talents. The same is the meaning of Kilavani, the Gujarati word for education. When we say that we develop a certain thing, it does not mean that we say that we develop a certain thing, it does not mean that we change its kind or quality, but that we bring out the qualities latent in it. Hence 'education' can also mean 'enfoldment'. In this sense, we cannot look upon knowledge of the alphabet as education. This is true even if that knowledge gains us the M.A. degree or enables us to adorn the place of a Shastri in some Pathshala with the requisite knowledge of Sanskrit. It may well that the highest literary knowledge is a fine instrument for education or enfoldment, but it certainly does not itself constitute education.

True education is something different. Man is made of those constituents, the body, mind and spirit. Of them, spirit is the one permanent element in man. The body and the mind function on account of it. Hence we can call that education which reveals the qualities of spirit. That is why the seal of the Vidyapith carries the dictum 'Education is that which leads to *moksha*'.

Education can also be understood in another sense; that is, whatever leads to a full or maximum development of all the three, the body, mind and spirit, may also be called education. The knowledge that is being imparted today may possibly develop the mind a little, but certainly it does not develop the body and spirit. I have a doubt about the development of the mind too, because it does not mean that the mind has developed if we have filled it with a lot of information. We cannot therefore say that we have educated our mind. A well-educated mind serves man in the desired manner. Our literate mind of today pulls us hither and thither. That is what a wild horse does. Only when a wild horse is broken in can we call it a trained horse. How many 'educated' young man of today are so trained?

Now let us examine our body. Are we supposed to cultivate the body by playing tennis, football or cricket for an hour every day? It does, certainly, build up the body. Like a wild horse, however, the body will be strong but not trained. A trained body is healthy, vigorous and sinewy. The hands and feet can do any desired work. A pickaxe, a shovel, a hammer, etc. are like ornaments to a trained hand and it can wield them. That hand can ply the spinning- wheel well as also the ring and the comb while the feet work a loom.

A well trained body does not get tired in trudging 30 miles. It can scale mountains without getting breathless. Does the student acquire such physical culture? We can assert that modern curricula do not impart physical education in this sense.

The less said about the spirit the better. Only a seer or a seeker can enlighten the soul. Who will awaken that dormant spiritual energy in us all? Teachers can be had through an advertisement. Is there a column for spiritual quest in the testimonials which they have to produce? Even if there is one, what is its value? How can we get through advertisements teachers who are seekers after self-realisation? And education without such enlightenment is like a wall without a foundation or, to employ an English saying, like a whited sepulcher. Inside it there is only a corpse eaten up or being eaten by insects. (Navajivan Education Supplement, 28 February 1926 (CW 30, pp. 58-59))

EDUCATION AND SOCIAL SYSTEM

Education as training

Now I have read a great deal in the prison. I have been reading Emerson, Ruskin, and Mazzini. I have also been reading the Upanishads. All confirm the view that education does not mean knowledge of letters but it means character building, it means knowledge of duty. Our own word literally means 'training'. If this be the true view and it is to my mind the only true view, you are receiving the best education-training-possible.

Education as service

True education lies in serving others; oblige them without the least feeling of one-uppishness. The more mature you grew, the more you will realize this. A great deal of religious obligation on us is fulfilled when we nurse the sick. I am not worried about your bookish learning so long as you perform your duties and observe solemn ethical conduct. For me carrying out the fundamentals of ethics is duty. I shall support you if you want to study further out of your love for it or for excellence. But I won't scold you if you do not do it. Try your best to carry out the decisions you have made. Write to me what you do at the press, at what time do you get up and about your work at the farm.

Education as liberation

"That is true education which leads to freedom." That alone is true education which enables us to preserve our dharma. This is the motto accepted by our university. The idea has appealed to me very much: "that is the true education which leads to freedom." That which liberates is education. Liberation is of two kinds. One form of liberation consists in securing the freedom of the country from foreign rule. Such freedom may prove short- lived. The other kind of liberation is for all time. In order to attain *moksha,* which we describe as our *paramadharma,* we should have freedom in the worldly sense as well. He who is ridden with many fears cannot attain the ultimate *moksha*. If one would attain this, would achieve the highest end of human effort, one has no choice but to attain that *moksha* which is nearest to one. That education which delays our freedom is to be shunned, it is Satanic, and it is sinful. Whatever the quality of the education given in government schools and colleges, it is to be shunned because the government which imparts it is Satanic and deserves to be shunned. (*Speech to students, Ahmadabad, 18 November 1926 (CW 18, P. 471)*)

Futures of Gandhi's Nai Talim

Nai Talim in Gandhi's vision has the following features as given below:

1. There would not be any strait-jacket framework or rigid structure of a Nai Talim system.
2. Nai Talim is closely related to social organization.
3. "Sharir- Parishram nishta" and Samya Yoga as Mantra, and root industries (Mool udyog) as its Tantras.

4. Old Talim (OT) differentiated between mental labour and "body labour". Nai Talim holds that both types of lobour have the same value; in fact, Nai Talim tries to integrate the two. Old-Talim appreciates capacity, competence, while Nai Talim regards capacity to be the means of equality.

5. It is time to accept that in education, we do not have to teach history, grammar, maths. We have to teach life.

6. The facilities for education, preparing text-books should be decentralized, and it will be such as will take into account the endowments of each village. The uniform books are hardly useful in education.

7. One of the fundamental tenets feed the body by doing intellectual work to do so is not a correct "Dharma". Sharir should be maintained by sharirshram only. This is a "bread labour" tenet of Nai Talim which underlies the roots of Nai Talim.

8. It must be grasped beyond any doubt that Nai Talim is not a reformed version of any other scheme or plan. It is an independent, free, special, radical, revolutionary idea.

9. Nai Talim means establishment of new values. Old Talim condemned stealing. Nai Talim condemns accumulation also.

10. In the regime of Nai Talim, self-dependence and Samyayga are like two lungs and they must be present in Nai Talim.

11. Nai Talim is not any modified western scheme, borrowed by us. It is very much an indigenous, free, unique system. It means establishment of new values. In this dispensation, the teacher would be a child; and child would be grown up.

12. In schools, prayers should be said daily and this should be done in Mother Tongue. Buniyadi Talim means Talim which is given to pupils in the beginning itself. Nai Talim is for everyone in the country. There is no need to think of separate Talims for every man and society. Our whole education would be based on Buniyad of Nai Talim. There is no difference in education for cities and villages. The Nai Talim is viewed as a system, a method, technique. It is a self-controlled system, it is not licentious system. It is like sea. The various rivers go and meet the ocean; similarly various thoughts may merge in it.

13. It is the creed of Nai Talim that knowledge and works (Karma) are one, they are not different from each other. When it is not possible to separate unity from duality to say that there is "Samavaya" in such

a relationship. The educational system in which Karma and *Dnan* are not distinguished from each other, we say that there is "Samavaya" between Karma and Dnan.

The relationship of Samavaya is expressed by Dhaneshwar in the following Marathi "Abhanga" very well.

"Tuja Saguna Mhanu Ki Nirguna re'I
Saguna Nirguna Eku Govindu re II

[O'Lord, shall I call you manifest, or shall I call you unmanifest

14. Nai Talim is a plan for giving bliss "Aanand" for 24 hours a day.
15. Nai Talim seeks to impart free and compulsory education for all boys and girls between the ages of seven and fourteen.
16. To impart education through some craft of productivework.
17. To impart self-supporting education.
18. To impart education through the mother tongue only.
19. To promote ideal citizenship.
20. To develop flexible curriculum, and to offer free environment to the students. The subject of the curriculum would be Basic craft, which may be spinning and weaving, carpentry agriculture, fruit and flower cultivation, leather works, cultures, fish, poultry, any handicraft according to the local need, and home science for girls.
21. Nai Talim removes the barrier between the educated and not educated, between manual work and intellectual work, between the rich and poor, and between the village and town.
22. Basic education is activity-centered; the child is not a passive learner bat an active participant in learning process. It fosters learning by doing.
23. Basic education is child-centric, and it harnesses constructive and creative instincts of the children.
24. It is truly an education for the cultural and social heritage of the land. Therefore, it inculcates social and moral values.
25. It is truly an education for the whole man. It aims at a harmonious development of the body, mind, and soul.
26. It recognizes the dignity of labour. It inculcates domestic values like co-operation, responsibility, fellow-feeling in students mind.
27. The scheme is economically and financially productive, it is based on the principles of work, and work occupies a central place in Nai Talim.

28. The system is capable of removing class and caste distinction. It can bring social solidarity and national integration.

29. The characteristics of Nai Talim are: Education is for liberation, freedom, sakshatkar and moksha.

30. Nai Talim talks about predominantly rural education in India; such an education is craft-oriented. The obsessive pursuit of knowledge is to be avoided.

31. In Nai Talim, spiritualism, socialism, and non-violence would have important place. The intellectual work should not be below 10 per cent per annum. This concept would favor increasing self-reliance and organic growth over speed of development and modernization.

32. In Nai Talim curriculum for different ages would be:

I. First seven years with stress on physical education.

II. 7 to 14 years for reading, writing and music. etc.

III. 14 to 21 years devoted to learning Arithmetic, biology, etc

IV. After 20 years of age, politics, religion, psychology, war and peace.

The Nai Talim holds that books are not necessary for teaching/ learning at least at the initial stage. The books are not only not necessary but they are harmful also. Gandhi objection to students making the use of books was on moral, ethical, and pratical (Vyavaharic) grounds. They were of the view that books are not necessary in the first year itself for learning subjects like geography, history, etc. the students will learn these subjects and poems in "Sahaj" way. They should not be required to cram alphabet, numbers etc.

Education as Assimilation

But I must advise you, students, to read these prize-books carefully, to reflect over their real import and, keeping in mind all the profound truths set out in them, follow the path enjoined by religion. Whether you are a girl or a boy, you will grow up one day and have to carry a heavy burden of worldly duties; give some thought, therefore, to the future. Truth is revealed not only in our scriptures but in the scriptures of other religions as well.

It is the duty of students to assimilate whatever they have learnt. They should have religious and moral instruction, as much of it as they can usefully apply. They need education in such measure that it would not become too much of a useless burden on them. I should like to address a few words exclusively to you have learnt only to the extent that you have assimilated it. That should be the object of this institution too. You should ponder over the element of truth in whatever books of religion you read. If you cling to truth, success is yours. I would advise you from my experience, to profit well from your education. That will be to advantage and to your counties as well. *(Speech to Students In Bombay, 14 February 1915 (CW 13, P.23))*

Education as Contemplation

Education, character and religion should be regarded as convertible terms. There is no true education which does not tend to produce character, and there is no true religion which does not determine character. Education should contemplate the whole life. Mere memorizing and book-learning is not education. I have no faith in so-called systems of education which produce men of learning without the backbone of character. *(Interview with W.W. Hall, October 1928 (CW 37, P.248))*

Education of the whole child

Education does not mean knowledge of the alphabet. This type of knowledge is only a means to education. Education implies a child's learning how to put his mind and his sense to good use. That is to say, he really learns how to use his hands, feet and other organs of action and his nose, ear and other organs of sense. A child who has acquired the knowledge that he should not use his hands for stealing or neither for killing flies nor for beating up his companions or younger brothers and sisters has already begun his education. He has started it, we can say, when he understands the necessity of keeping his body, his teeth, tongue, ears, head, nails, etc., clean and keeps them clean. That child has made good progress in education who does not indulge in mischief while eating and drinking, eats and drinks alone or in society in a proper manner, sits properly and chooses pure foodstuffs knowing the difference between pure and impure foodstuffs, does not eat like a glutton, does not clam our for whatever he sees and remains clam even if he gets what he wants.

Even that child has advanced on the road to education whose pronunciation is correct, who can recount to us the history and geography of the country surrounding him without knowing those terms and who understands what his country means. That child has made very good progress in his education who can understand the difference between truth and untruth, worth and worthlessness and chooses the good and the true, while rejecting the bad and the untrue. *(Navajivan, 2 June 1929 (CW 41, P. 6))*

Education as self-discipline

All your scholarship, all your study of Shakespare and Wordsworth would be Vain if at the same time you do not build your character, and attain mastery over your thoughts and actions. When you have attain self-mastery and learnt to control your passions you will not utter notes of despair. You cannot give your hearts and process poverty of action. To give once heart is to give all. You must, to start with, have hearts to give. And this you can do if you will cultivate them. *(Speech to Students, Agra, 19 September 1929(CW 41, 391))*

Education and culture

"Culture" means refinement of feelings and "education" means knowledge of literature. Education is a means and culture is the end. The latter is possible even without education. For instance, if a child is brought in a cultural family, it will unconsciously imbibe culture from its environment. In our country at any rate, present-day education and culture have no connection with each other. If the educated still retain some culture that is in spite of their education. This fact shows that the root of our culture is deep (*Letter to Premabehn kantak-5 January 1931 (CW 74, P.422))*

Knowledge of the self

True education is that which helps us to know the *atman,* our true self, God and truth. To acquire this knowledge, some persons may feel the need for a study of literature, some for a study of physical sciences and some others for art. But every branch of knowledge should have as its goal knowledge of the self. That is so in the Ashram. We carry on numerous activities with that aim in view. All of them are, in my sense of the term, true education. Those activities can also be carried on without any reference to the goal of knowledge of the self. When they are so carried on, they may serve as a means of livelihood or of something else, but they are not education. In an activity carried on as education, a proper understanding of its meaning, devotion to duty and the spirit of the service are necessary. (10 July 1932 (CW 50 P. 182))

Ideal education

When it is remembered that the primary aim of all education is, or should be, the moulding of the character of the pupils, a teacher who has a character to keep need not lose heart. *(Harijan, 1 December 1933, P. 3 (CW 56, P. 296))*

Real education

Real education has to draw out the best from the boys and the girls to be educated. This can never be done by packing ill-assorted and unwanted information in to the heads of the pupils. It becomes a dead weight crushing all originality in them and turning them into mere automata *(Harijan, 1 December 1933, P. 3 (CW 56, P. 295))*

Book of humanity

Real education consists in drawing the best out of yourself. What better book can there be then the book of humanity. *(Harijan, 30 March 1934, P. 55)*

Education of the hand

Literary education should follow the education of the hand the one gift that visibly distinguishes man from beast. It is a superstition to think that the fullest development of man is impossible without knowledge of the art of reading and writing. That knowledge undoubtedly adds grace to life, but is in no way indispensable for man's moral, physical, or material growth. *(Harijan, 8 March 1935, P. 28)*

Education for a new world

Education must be of a new type the sake of the creation of a new world. *(Harijan, 19 January 1947, P. 494)*

GANDIAN AIMS, IMPORTANCE AND OBJECTIVES OF BASIC EDUCATION

GANDIAN EDUCATION AIMS

Gandhis concept of education has twofold aims before it-immediate and ultimate.

Immediate aims of education:-

Certain immediate aims of Gandhis concept of education are concerned with our day-to-day life. Immediate aims of education according to Gandhiji are as under:-

1) **Bread and Butter Aim (vocational Aim):-** Gandhiji believes that a poor country like India where earning of bread is the main problem, educations must aim at enabling every individual to earn his livelihood. It must enable him to stand on one's own feet. In the words of Gandhiji, "Education ought to be for them (children) a kind of insurance against unemployment".

2) **Cultural Aim:** - Gandhiji could never admit vocational as the end of life. Therefore, he also paid attention to culture. In the words of Gandhiji, "I attach more importance to cultural factor of education than its literary factor. Culture is a primary and basic thing which the girls should receive from school".

From this point of view, Gandhiji regarded the cultural aim of education as an important aim. The cultural aim lays emphasis on obtaining knowledge of Indian culture- the culture that is reflected in our dress, our manner of speech, our way of conduct and our behaviour. Education, with the cultural aim, will liberate the soul from pride, prejudice and encumbrances and enable man to see things in their true perspective.

3) **Character Aim:** - Gandhiji regarded character formation as the suitable foundation of education. Hence the end of all knowledge must be building up of character. He regarded the character as the expression of the whole personality including its ethical and spiritual aspect. Character building implies the cultivation of such moral virtues as courage, strength of conviction, righteousness, and purity in personal life, self-restraint and service of humanity. According to Gandhiji, education without character and character devoid of purity would be no good.

4) **Perfect Development Aim:** - The child's all-around and perfect development aim is the sole aim. An all-round development means the development of the head, heart and hand-nothing less, nothing more. "Man is neither mere intellect, nor the gross animal body, nor heart or soul alone. A proper and harmonious contribution of all the three is required for the making of the whole man and is the true economics of education". Gandhiji states. "True education is that which draws out and stimulates the spiritual, intellectual and physical faculties of the children".

Ultimate aim of education:-

Self-realization or Summum Bonum is the ultimate aim of life as well as education. Spiritual freedom provides knowledge of God and Self-realization. Hence education should provide spiritual freedom.

According to Gandhiji, "development of the moral character, development of the whole- all were directed towards the realization of the ultimate reality- the merger of the finite being into the infinite.

Harmonious Blending of individual and social Aim:-

Gandhiji advocated both individual and social aims of education at different times. He did not find any conflict between the two. In fact, he believed in the synthesis of the two. He thought the if individuals are good; the whole society shall be good. According to him, if we succeed in building the character of the individual, society will take care of itself. On the other hand, he also said that the state or the society should also be good and try to save the individuals. He always loved individual freedom but he regarded individuals as social creatures. He thought that the development of personality is impossible in loneliness. In the words of Mahatma Ghandi, "A nation cannot advance without the units of which it is composed and conversely, an individual cannot advance without the nation of which he is a part".

Gandhi's ideal of self-realization combines both the development of individuality as well as the society. No person can be said to have achieved self-realization unless he is fully conscious of the social needs and tries to fulfill them.

Gandian education objectives

I. Physical development: According to the educational philosophy of M. Ghandi education should be such that the child's body should develop since a healthy mind is farmed in a healthy body that is why he emphasized physical development first.

II. Mental and intellectual development: According to Gandhiji, just as a child needs mother's milk for physical development, in the same way, education is needed for mental development.

III. Personal and social development: Gandhiji emphasizes the development of individuals, society, and nations. Social development means that spiritual development is possible only by loving human beings in society and serving human begins.

IV. Cultural development: Gandhiji laid special emphases on the need for knowledge of culture for spiritual development, according to him; culture has an important role in education philosophy. V. Moral and character development: According to Gandhiji education philosophy, the qualities of truth, non-violence, celibacy, tastelessness, non-possession and dependence etc should be developed in the child.

V. Professional development: Gandhiji used to emphasize vocational education for the freedom of economic development and wants to make man, self-reliant, that is why he emphasized handicraft and industry.

VI. Spiritual development: Gandhiji considers liberation and self-realization as the ultimate objective of human life. Gandhiji lays equal emphasis on knowledge, action, devotion and yoga; it gives the embodiment of non-violence and Satyagraha.

IMPORTANCE

(i) Free and Compulsory Primary Education:

Gandhiji envisaged seven years free, compulsory and universal primary education up to matriculation minus English. In other words, he wanted to combine the present primary and secondary education into one—called the English-less matriculation. It should be free because India is a poor country and all the parents cannot afford the cost of education.

It should be compulsory because majority of people do not realize the central value of education in life and do not send their wards o the school. Therefore, he wanted to make education compulsory for all so that the children may attend the school regularly rather than attending some other duties assigned by their ignorant and illiterate parents.

Moreover, nobody would be denied to receive education up to 14 years of age. As such, it is universal in nature.

(ii) Craft-centred Education:

Craft-centred education is not education plus crafts but it is education through craft. Craft is the nucleus of education. It is the centre of the entire teaching-learning process. Education in a sense should be centred on some productive craft. It is this education through which all-round development of the child can be possible.

He said, "It was his wish that, the whole process of education should be imparted through some handicraft or industry." Further he added that the handicraft should not be taught mechanically but scientifically which implies that the child should know the why and wherefore of every process.

For example, by teaching Takli-Spinning, knowledge of different varieties of cotton, the different soils in different pockets of India, the history of the decay of handicraft, a knowledge of Arithmetic etc. should be imparted. The craft should not be taught merely for production work but for developing the intellect of the pupils.

His object was not to produce craftsmen but he wanted to exploit it for educative purposes. He wanted that stress should be laid on the principles of co-operative activity, planning, accuracy, initiative and individual responsibility in learning.

He outlined the following factors as regards to the selection of craft:

a) It should be the centre around which the different subjects can be clubbed,

b) It should find natural point? of correlation with important activities and interests,

c) It must be according to the natural and social environment

d) It should be tied with the life of the children,

e) It should meet the vocational needs of the child in the changing social order.

Craft-centred education is significant on the following scores:

(a) It is psychologically sound as it relieves the child from the tyranny of a purely academic, theoretical and monotonous instruction. It is a means of fostering the power of imagination and sharpening the intellect. It gives wide scope to children for self-expression by sublimation of their instincts.

Moreover, the psychological needs of the children i.e. need for affection, self-respect, creativeness are fulfilled through craft-centred education.

(b) It is sociologically sound as the introduction of practical productive work can break down the hiatus between urban and rural life when it tends to infuse a sense of dignity of labour in the children. It breaks the existing wall of prejudice between manual and intellectual work. It brings a sense of co-operation, discipline, belongingness, tolerance and self-government in children.

(c) Economically, it is considered as sound as it increases the productive capacity of our workers and also enables them to utilize their leisure advantageously. It also helps in attaining the aim of self-supporting aspect of education.

(d) It is pedagogically sound since it gives reality to knowledge. It helps to bring correlation of knowledge with life and its various aspects.

(e) From the biological stand-point, it is sound as it provides opportunities for earning while learning.

Self-Sufficiency:

It implies that the child should be able to cover some part of his educational expenses by engaging himself in some productive works which would give him earning along with learning. It also enables the child to earn a living after completing his course of education—preparing the child for future life.

Secondly, education imparted in it should be self-supporting to an extent that the productive work of the pupils would meet the expenses of the school viz, salaries of the teachers, expenditure on raw-materials and maintenance of equipment and furniture.

Gandhiji realized that a poor nation like India that cannot provide education to all the pupils free of cost which necessitates education to be self-supporting and self-sufficient.

His self-sufficiency aspects were criticized on the grounds of the following:

a) Critics thought that by indulging children in productive works, school would exploit them. It was nothing but exploitation of the child labour. Therefore, the tender age of children is grossly exploited and spoiled.

b) Some develops fear that if children are left free in making goods, they would mishandle the machinery which would cause irreparable loss. Thus, there would be enormous waste at the hands of small children.

c) It was thought that child would use all his energy and power for earning money and in the process of earning child would neglect his study. Thus, learning of the child would be atrophied.

d) Critics argue that parents would reap the advantage of child labour by propelling the child to do some works in the hope of shunning their onus.

e) Lastly, it was thought that children might produce articles which could not compete with the marketable articles produced in factories because their products were very rough and crude.

In-spite of its drawbacks, craft-centred education is unique for its self-sufficiency aspect which brings about economic prosperity.

(iii) Emphasis on Mother-tongue:

He realized that the greatest handicap of the prevailing system of education was that learning was being imparted through the medium of English. This affected the development of understanding, precision of thought and clarity of ideas. Mother tongue, on the contrary, would enable the children to understand clearly the rich heritage of people's ideas, emotions and aspirations, to express freely, clearly and lucidly in speaking and writing, to use the list of contents and the indices, and to consult dictionaries and reference books.

(iv) Correlation as a Method of Teachings:

It was envisaged that correlation should be the guiding principle of teaching all subjects. Different subjects are to be taught making craft as the focal point of teaching-learning process. Gandhiji wanted an effective and natural correlation between the craft and other subjects and the co-ordination of various subjects.

For example, in Geography teaching, it can be correlated with spinning through a thread-bare discussion on the nature of soil required for plantation of cotton, climatic condition, period of vegetation etc. In language teaching, it can be done by stimulating pupils to write an essay on cotton.

In Science subject, pupils can be asked to make a nature study for the growth of the cotton plants. Therefore, it is the starting point of teaching all other subjects and it is the medium through which different subjects are to be taught effectively by means of correlation. As such, he had distaste towards water tight compartmentalization of manifold subjects.

(v) Creed of Non-violence:

A very outstanding feature of his educational philosophy was the application of the law of Ahimsa in the training of the child as a prospective world citizen. He thought that non-violence was the panacea for all evils.

He said, "Where the whole atmosphere is redolent with the pure fragrance of ahimsa, boys and girls studying together will have like brothers and sisters in freedom and yet in self-imposed restraint; the students will be bound to the teachers in ties of filial love, mutual respects and mutual trust."

His scheme of education wanted to establish a society free from communal hat redness and all forms of and exploitation. His plan of education was based upon the pillar of non-violence (Ahimsa). His aim was to evolve a non-violent society based on love, mutual respect, sympathy and co-operation through education.

(vi) Ideal of citizenship:

Gandhiji wanted to make children right type of citizens endowed with civic sense, conscious of one's own duties and rights, responsibilities and opportunities. This would be possible by his new indigenous system of education. Education should, therefore, be directed to conform to this standard of citizenship.

(vii) Freedom from Bondage

You have asked for my blessings. Then you certainly have, but you have them on the condition that you impart luster to this Vidyalaya and its name. The patidars also should benefit by it and should disagree neither the vallabh Vidyalaya which may prove a millstone round my neck and be a burden to me. Education liberates us, frees us from bondage, helps us to shine, adds to the country's wealth, and enriches character: our boys and girls become smart and intelligent thereby. This Vidyalaya has been established with this end in view. May this end be realized? *(Speech at Vallabh Vidyalaya Buchanan, 10 May 1931 (CW 46, p. 101))*

National character

What is your goal in education when India obtains self-rule?

Character building, I would try to develop courage, strength, virtue, the ability to forget oneself in working towards great aims. This is more important than literacy; academic learning is only a means to this greater end. That is why Indin's great lack of literacy, deplorable as it is, does not appeal to me nor make me feel that India is unfit for self-rule.

Would you try to bring about any specific kind of social organization through education?

I would feel that if we succeed in building the character of the individual, society will take care of itself. I would be quite willing to trust the organization of society to individuals so developed.

In developing the new national spirit in India would you like to make patriotic feelings so strong that duty to one's country would be a higher good them obeying one's personal conscience?

I hope that will never be. One's own inner convictions come first always. But in a nation where character is developed in all individuals, there can be no conflict between the dictates of one's own conscience and those of the state. (Remakers of Mankind, 1932, pp.104-05)

Developing independent thinking

At present, the minds of the students become dull there. They can only imitate. Instead of this, they must acquire the power of independent thinking. We are born into this world not for indulging in sensuous activities but for sacrifice, for restraint, the purpose of education is that we know God and progress towards the ideal, and get closer to him. It is the strict law of God that anyone who desires to be close to him should renounce the world and yet be in it. This is what the first *mantra* of the *ishopanished* exhorts us to do. This thing is difficult and yet easy at the same time. Is easy if we believe that we have to live for service. We acquire learning not for sensuous pleasures and for earning but for *mukti*. Education is considered necessary to save ourselves from darkness, sensuous pleasures and capricious behaviour. *(Speech at students meeting, Lahore, 13 July 1934 (CW 58, p. 183))*

CURRICULUM AND METHODS OF TEACHING

Curriculum

Arithmetic: Arithmetic should be correlated with life situations. The various processes of arithmetic should be correlated with the basic crafts. He also considered that arithmetic is a very useful subject for day to day life.

Social studies: Gandhiji wanted that children should acquire knowledge of social studies including history, geography, civics and current events for promoting the status of an individual.

General sciences: General sciences viz. zoology, physiology, chemistry, botany and Astronomy should be taught for promoting intelligent and scientific outlooks. Domestic science should also be added for the girls in fourth and fifth classes.

Music and Drawing: These subjects should be included for creating the real interest in education.

Basic crafts: Basis crafts including agriculture, spinning, weaving, wood work, gardening and leader work should be included in accordance with local conditions of life and society. Gandhiji asserted that education should be craft centered and hence craft has a primary place in Gandhis system of education.

Mother tongue: He emphasized that the mother tongue is to be used as the medium of instruction in the schools because mother tongue is an effective medium for expression and communication of ideas.

METHODS OF TEACHING

Gandhiji has given important place to the following principles and methods under the teaching methods:

I. **"Learning by proper use of Body Organs:** Gandhiji believes that true education to the mind can be got only by proper exercise of body organs, as hands, eye, nose, etc. and teaching. In other words, the rational use of body organs is the most suitable and rapid way of developing a child's mind. Gandhiji says that a child should be taught drawing at first, and then reading and identifying the letters of alphabet, only then he should be taken to writing.

II. **Learning by Doing:** Gandhiji has emphasized on learning by doing in his teaching method, so he has taken crafts as the centre of his basic education. It provides abundant opportunities to a child for learning by doing. From social viewpoint also, this method develops the qualities of cooperation, sympathy and sociality, etc. Learning by doing, as against from teacher, leaves a permanent mark on the mind. The opportunity to learn by self-experience is dependent on activity.

III. **Learning by Synthesis:** Gandhiji has understood the importance of the principle of correlation as lay down by psychology, and has supported the method of making every useful-for-life education as industry-oriented. He says in this context that basic handicrafts should be in the form of a full circle and other subjects should revolve round it like planets and get energy or light from the central sun.

IV. **Learning by Reading, Thinking and Action**: Gandhiji has accepted the three levels of Indian way of learning (hearing, thinking and meditation) as reading, thinking and action. He says that all these three should exist in a teaching method. If knowledge is acquired in the absence of any of them, then it would be temporary and useless.

V. **Learning by Experiment:** there is much scope for practical work in Gandhiji basic education plan. By this method, a child can study the cause of origin of different problems, their present state, and form and can comprehend them. Each level can be tested to estimate its scientific relativity and social importance, and adopt it in practical life to acquire its knowledge accordingly."

Gandhi has written practically on every aspect of human life and his writings particularly on education are full of incisive insight, practical experience and pragmatic foresight. Gandhi's experiment in India and presents his thoughts on various stages of education from primary to higher education. The richness of his ideas on language learning, women's education, physical education and almost other aspects of learning provide an insight into the vastness of his vision and the expense of his thought process. He was a practical idealistic.

EXPERIMENTS IN CHAMPARAN SCHOOLS

South Africa

Durban, 1897, Gandhi did not send his children to European schools because of his disbelief in English medium education. He himself taught them through their mother-tongue Gujarati.

Phoenix settlement

South Africa, 1904, Gandhi started a school in South Africa with 30 children. Institution was given both in literary aspects and training in agriculture and painting. It was an ideal school-workshop wherein both theory and practice were integrated.

Tolstoy Farm

Transvaal, 1911, this was an ashram set up with the help and guidance of Hermann Kallenach, a German co-worker. People belonging to various religions- Hindus, Muslims, Parsis, Christians- lived together. Some Hindu girls were also there. More importance was given to culture of the heart and character building. Even physical culture was emphasized through cooking, scavenging and gardening. Learning was to be a joyous adventure and teachers were expected to set an example.

Champaran

Champaran was the land of indigo plantations. Indigo plants were grown and indigo was manufactured in Champaran at great hardship to thousands of farmers. Champaran was situated in Bihar. Accepting the invitation of the cahmparan farmers to see for himself the anguish of those indigo farmers, Gandhi set out for the place in 1917. Gandhi realized that Bihar was a place of strict untouchability and it was deeply painted. Gandhi was touched by the humility, simplicity, goodness and extraordinary faith. Of those farmers whose problems overwhelmed him. Gandhi's aim, first of all, was to thoroughly inquire into the condition of the Champaran farmers and understand their grievances against the indigo planters. Gandhi was faced with difficulties chiefly from the side of officials and indigo planters whose vested interest in the affairs was a significant factor. Gandhi was ordered to leave Champaran and was threatened with arrest. But the officials soon realized that people were with Gandhi, that he did not have any personal grievances but only wised to offer civil resistance to their orders. Gandhi recalls, "The people had for the moment lost all fear of punishment and yielded obedience to the power of love which their new friend exercised". All that was inspite of the fact that no one in Champaran knew Gandhi except a few of his close associates who led him to the place. They did not know the Congress and no political work was done among them. For Gandhi that meeting with the Champaran farmers was a face to face confrontation with God. Ahimsa and Truth. Gandhi was finally permitted by the Authorities to proceed with inquiry and they promised him all the necessary help he needed for the inquiry. The first stage of Gandhi's mission in Champaran ended successfully.

Gandhi's acquaintance with the problems of Bihar convinced him that a change of a permanent nature was not possible without educate village education. Ignorance and poverty reigned supreme everywhere. The workers led a pathetic life with no possibility to rise above and understand their true plight. Everybody toiled for a meager wage and it was just a matter of existence for the workers in the plantation. Gandhi made his own plans to improve their lot. He opened primary schools in six villages. The poverty in those villages was so utter that no money could be raised for the purpose of establishing those schools. The thing they could do was to contribute grain and other raw-materials.

It was difficult for Gandhi to provide teachers for those schools, especially when they would have to work on a minimum salary or without remuneration at all. Gandhi never liked the idea of employing just ordinary teachers for doing a work which he knew was crucial to the development of those villages. In response to a public appeal Gandhi issued, there came immense response from various quarters to have teacher sent to Champaran for the work.

Primary education could be only a beginning. The whole village was wanting in education in hygienic habits. Wherever Gandhi went he was confronted with dirt and filth to unbearable dimensions. The homes were kept most untidy, the lanes full of dirt, wells which were the nerve-centre of the village could be seen surrounded with mud and filth. Skin diseases were mist common with elderly people.

Education could not be conceived of as an isolated thing in Champaran. If education meant the welfare of the villagers it had to be integrated with health and sanitation. The group launched a medical help-drive in all the villages under the supervision of the doctor in the group to meet the medical needs of the villagers and ensure basic health in them. Self-help even in this regard was a thing unheard of among them. They were willing to do nothing to improve their health and surroundings.

Education through village sanitation was proved a difficult affair. The children were given instructions about cleanliness and general sanitation in classes. But the problems lay with adults; they were not willing to do anything by themselves. Even field laborers were not willing undertake cleaning up their surroundings. The volunteers, therefore, concentrated on the village an ideal place to live in. They swept the roads and the courtyards cleaned out the wells, filted up the pools nearby, and lovingly persuaded the villagers to raise volunteers from among themselves.

At several place the villagers frankly expressed their dislike for the work Gandhi did. That was simply to be expected because of the dire habits the villagers had formed by living under adverse conditions. Inspite of that it was possible for the volunteers in Champaran to touch the hearts of the villagers with their work in school, sanitation work and medical relief. Gandhi wanted a permanent group of volunteers to carry on the work he had started in Champaran. But that did not materials for want of people. The educational work became a part of Gandhi's experiment in that direction. That was an attempt to challenge the traditional mode of literary education by imparting to little children facts about things which hardly come under their usual, day-to-day experience. The work in Champaran was an example as to how problems in typical rural India could be dealt with.

National Schools

Gandhi's vision for national schools as the tools for the attainment of Swaraj consisted of communal unity, propagating the significance of charkha and abolishing the curse of untouchability. Spinning was a symbol of laboring for the country, patriotism and useful toil. Gandhi aimed at the revival of cottage industry by introducing spinning and craft making as methods of education. Gandhi also insisted on imparting such education through one's mother-tongue, making it a vehicle of one's thoughts and ideas. He emphasized the manual and industrial training, thus making it 'an intelligent approach, a more valuable aid to the intellect than an indifferent reading of literature' (Young India, 21-6-1928). Gandhi's proposals in the Wardha conference were a blueprint for the national basic education system.

Gujarat Vidyapith

The 'National University of Gujarat' or Gujarat Vidyapith, as is popularly known, was established in 1920 and serves as a perfect example of a National University as visualized by Gandhi. It was a protest against British injustice, and a vindication of national honour. As Gandhi said, 'it draws its inspiration from the national ideals of a united India'. It aimed at the 'unique ideal of achieving a united India shedding all the caste and communal differences' (Mukalel, p.101). With a highly value-oriented education as its base, the university became the centre of Indian Vedic culture and education, and fostered the students as Satyagraha in the process of attaining Swaraj and future nation-building. Gandhi himself taught the students and explained the significance of all religions. Gandhi envisioned the university as a symbol of nationalist ideas and wanted other universities to emulate the Vidyapith

EXPERIMENTS ON TRUTH

Gandhi's Experiments with Truth of all the great world figures Gandhi emerges to be unique because of his approach to life. There has been no one who exercised such tremendous energy to arrive at a close synthesis of the ideals and principles of life and the practical, day-to-day living at the grass-root level. Gandhi says, "Experience of the soul is the richest and the only one that helps our development". He was most willing to keep before his eyes the significance of right from the minute details of life up to the final goal of Self-realization. Gandhi observed life and its movements like a magician observing his magic crystal for best results. Gandhi was an idealist and be proved himself to be a committed pragmatist.

Gandhi viewed life as the arena for the recognition and realization of truth. For Gandhi "Truth is more fundamental than atom itself". Truth is hidden in the vast reservoir of life which the individual is out to discover. Truth is like an ice-berg whose tiny edge alone is seen on surface: the individual is oriented to discover the gigantic portions of it hidden beneath the waters of life. Gandhi's unique method of discovering this vast reservoir and this gigantic ice-berg of truth constituted his experiments with truth and life. Gandhi was convinced that the more one searches deep into its realm the greater the discoveries one is bound to make. He says, "Truth is like a vast tree which yields more and more fruit, the more you nurture it".

Gandhi's unfailing dedication, keen observation and sense of commitment to the very caused helped him in this process of discrimination. This aspect was evident from Gandhi's experiment .In spirituality and education at the phoenix settlement, Tolstoy Farm and Sabarmati Ashram. Gandhi never saw life as black and white formula with a single proposed solution. He accepted the too complex nature of the reality of life and attempted to respond to the problems of life keeping this complexity in mind.

Gandhi was right in stressing the point that man requires a powerful motivation to follow his ideals, and the attraction of ideals needs to persist in order to keep his efforts going in the right direction. That was the strength working behind all his experiments. That was the strength Gandhi wants to work in the case of our experiments with life and education.

Gandhi's experiments with truth took manifold dimensions as a way of life to confront divinity in work ship and to confront his neighbor in live. Gandhi's experiments in diet keeping lead to further and further simple food habits in which he reaped wonderful results. In his opinion many such experiments taught me that the real of taste was not the tongue, but the mind. Gandhi's experiment with diet keeping and those to develop self-denial went hand-in-hand.

Gandhi's experiments with truth became in course of time experiments in simple life and a life of total self-dependency. That was Gandhi's antithesis to the over sophistication of his own times. He was governed by the powerful conviction that self-restraint alone could redeem mankind from catastrophy and the nation from slavery. He exhorts teachers, "A stranger to self-restraint could never teach his pupils the value of self-restraint. In all his experiments the basic fact was the search for the truth content that as we have seen had to be uncovered as part of the huge hidden ice-berg. He says, "I am a searcher after truth. My experiments hold to be infinitely more important than the best equipped Himalayan expeditions. And the result? If the search is scientific, surely there is no comparison between the two". Gandhi's greatness lies not only in his achievements but also the method and techniques he employed in every detailed approach of life.

NATIONALIST EXPERIMENTS IN EDUCATION

The education that was imparted only covered one aspect, literacy. It never attempted to harmonies the child's personality, by achieving a proper integration of the training of the mind body and spirit. Our villagers put in hard labor like animals and slaves. The education that was planned could not come down to their level and redeem then from that bondage to hard labour and poverty. They have gone down to the level animals without obtaining any help to develop their mind and spirit. Education is schools and colleges looked upon with respect because such an education was totally alienated from manual work and physical labour. Since form of exercise for the body was necessary schools introduced quit artificial and uninteresting physical training whole thing is ridiculous beyond words.

Gandhi felt that as nation we are so backward in education, and we have great obligation to the nation in this regard. He therefore in all force recommended that education should be made self-supporting. In the july issue of harijan (1937) Gandhi drew up his definition of education: "By education I mean all round drawing out best in child and man body mind and spirit". Literacy not the end of education, not even the beginning. Gandhi could not accommodate the idea that literacy was essentially education. He wanted to begin the child's education by teaching it a useful handicraft and by enabling it to produce from the moment it begins its training. So every school could be made self- supporting.

Gandhi held that the highest development of the mind and the soul was possible under such a system of education. Every handicraft had to be taught not merely mechanically, but in scientific manner proving the necessary intellectual stimulation. The method was adopted and tested out at several places wherever spinning and weaving were taught to workers. Gandhi taught sandal- making and spinning on these lines with good results. That method also included knowledge of history and geography. It meant all round development all round economy.

WARDHA EDUCATION CONFERENCE

Gandhi's new approach to education became craft-centered and skill-based, developed against the background of the concrete needs of the country. The new conception was also based on the education principles of John Dewey, who defines the school as a place "where experiments in life will be carried on where other experiments in life will be read about and told about because of their result". Gandhi was familiar with the pragmatist educational principle of learning by doing or learning through one's experience. Gandhi was thoroughly misunderstood as many thought that he was recommending sheer manual work as an alternative to all other studies. It became therefore a responsibility for him to discuss at length matters pertaining to his new concept of basic education.

A session of the Educational conference commenced at Wardha on 2nd. October 1937 served distinguished members of the congress including Dr.Zakir Hussain and Aryanayakam participated at the conference. Gandhi presented a review of his entire scheme of Education in his presidential address at the conference. Gandhi claimed the scheme of education to be fresh and new; although based on his experiences. Gandhi's ideas concerted education at the primary and college levels. He stressed the role it primary education that included in his conception the upper middle and then secondary also because he had grave concerns for the people in Indian villages and the primary education pertained to the villages more. He said that he was convinced of the need of to thus combine the primary and secondary education in just one stream to meet the requirement of rural conditions. Such a national scheme of education as what the conference had in mind had to be primarily for the villages.

Gandhi's scheme meant the teaching of the whole art and science as a craft and imparting the education as a practical training with orientations for adequate intellectual stimulation. Spinning becomes the starting point of a variety of subjects with elementary knowledge in them. Gandhi was convinced that spinning was the only practical solution to our problem, considering the grave economic situation that prevailed in India. Gandhi wanted primary education to centre on the 'takli'. During the first year everything could be taught through spinning. In the second year other processes could be introduced side by children could meet the requirements of parents themselves. It was seven year course leading to a practical knowledge of spinning, weaving, dyeing and designing. This primary education included also principles of sanitation, hygiene, nutrition, of doing their own work, helping parents at home etc. There would also be compulsory physical education through musical drill.

Gandhi concluded the address by inviting the attention of the conference to the fundamentals of self-supporting education. Our students are to be made true representatives of our culture and our civilization, of the true genius of our nation. Gandhi stressed the point that the whole western civilization' and its achievements were based on force and violence.

The conference was entrusted with the task of reviewing the proposals made in Gandhi's basic scheme. The proposals contained the following: 1. English, having been made the medium of instruction in universities, had created gap between the highly educated few and the uneducated many. It has prevented from knowledge from percolating to the masses. The absence of vocational training has made the educated class unfit for productive work and has harmed them physically. 2. The course of primary education would be extended at to seven years and should include the general knowledge gained up to the matriculation standard except English, and a vocation. 3. All the training should as far as possible is centered on a craft for the all-around development of the boys and girls. This primary education should equip the boys and girls to earn their bread and the state should guarantee employment in the vocations they are trained in. 4. Higher education should be left to private enterprise, and for the meeting of national requirements. The state universities should be purely examining bodies, self-supporting through the fees charged for the examinations.

The committee drew its draft resolutions and passed them the following day:

1. Free and compulsory education is provided for seven years on a nationwide scale.
2. The medium of instruction should be in the mother-tongue.
3. The process of education through our period should be centered on some form of manual of productive work and all other abilities to be developed and be integrated to the craft.
4. This system of education expected in course time to cover the remuneration of teachers.

Shantiniketan

From Rajkot, I proceeded to Shantiniketan. The teachers and students overwhelmed me with affection. The reception was a beautiful combination of simplicity, art and love.

The Phonex family had been assigned separate quarters at Shantiniketan. Maganlal Gandhi was at their head, and he had made it his business to see that all the rules of the phonex Ashram should be scrupulously observed. I saw that, by dint of his love, knowledge and perseverance, he had made his fragrance felt in the whole of Shantiniketan.

Andrews was there, and also Pearson. Amongst the Bengali teachers with whom we came in fairly close contact were Jagadanandbabu, Nepalbabu, Santoshbabu, Kshitimohanbabu, Nagenbabu, Sharadbabu and Kalibabu.

As is my wont, I quickly mixed with the teachers and students, and engaged them in a discussion on self-help. I put it to the teachers that, if they and the boys dispensed with the services of paid cooks and cooked their food themselves, it would enable the teachers to control the kitchen from the point of view the boy's physical and moral health, and it would afford to the students an object-lesson in self-help. One or two of them were inclined to share their heads. Some of them strongly approved of the proposal. The boys welcomed it, if only because of their instinctive taste for novelty. So we launched the experiment. When I invited the poet to express his opinion, he said that he did not mind it provided the teachers were favorable. To the boys he said, 'the experiment contains the key to Swaraj'.

Pearson began to wear away his body in making the experiment a success. He threw himself into it with zest. A batch was formed to cut vegetables, another to clean the grain, and so on. Nagenbabu and others undertook to see the sanitary cleaning of the kitchen and its surroundings. It was a delight to me to see them working spade in hand.

But it was too much to except the hundred and twenty-five boys with their teachers to take to this work of physical labour like ducks to water. There used to be daily discussion. Some began early to show fatigue. But Pearson was not the man to be tired. One would always find him with his smiling face doing something or other in or about the kitchen. He had taken upon himself the cleaning of the bigger utensils. A party of students played on their sitar before the cleaning party in order to beguile the tedium of the opinion. All alike took the thing up with zest and Shantiniketan became a busy hive.

Changes like these when once begun always develop. Not only was the phoenix party's kitchen self-conducted, but the food cooked in it was of the simplest. Condiments were eschewed. Rice, Dal, vegetables and even wheat flour were all cooked at one and the same time in a steam cooker. And Shantiniketan boys started a similar kitchen with a view to introducing reform in the Bengali kitcen. One or two teachers and some students ran this kitchen.

The experiment was, however, dropped after some time. I am of opinion that the famous institution lost nothing by having conducted the experiment for a brief interval, and some of the experiences gained could not but be of help to the teachers. *(An Autobiography Vol. II, p.565)*

Satyagraha Ashram, Kochrab

The Ashram experiment in education was a trial for us as nothing else was.

We saw at once that the women and children in the Ashram should be taught to read and write, and a little later on that there should be similar facilities for even the illiterate men that came to the Ashram. Those who had already joined the Ashram could not undertake to teach. If capable teachers were to be attracted to the Ashram, the rule of Brahmacharya had to be relaxed in their case. The Ashram was therefore divided into two sections, the 'teachers' quarters and the Ashram proper.

Human beings cannot overcome their weakness all at once. As soon as the two sections came into being, a feeling of superiority and inferiority poisoned the Ashram atmosphere in spite of all our efforts to scotch it. The Ashramites develop spiritual pride, which the teachers could not tolerate. The pride was an obstacle in the attainment of the Ashram ideal and therefore an aspect of untruth as well. But the brahmacharies had no reason to think too highly of themselves. It may be that the brahmacharis who sinned mentally in spite of themselves were retrogressing while those who did not claim to be brahmacharis but liked brahmacharya were making progress. This was clear to the intellect but it was not easy for all of us to put it into practice.

Then again there were differences of opinion as regards the method of education which gave rise to difficulties in administration. There were bitter discussions, but at last all calmed down and learned the lesson of forbearance. This was in my view a triumph of truth, the goal of all Ashram Endeavour. Those who held divergent views harbourted no evil intentions in their minds, and were indeed grieved at the divergence. They wished to practice truth as they saw it. Their partially for their own standpoint came in the way of their giving due weight to the arguments of their opponents. Hence the quarrels which put our charity to a severe test.

I have my own perhaps peculiar views on education which have not been accepted by my colleagues in full, and here they are:

1. Young boys and girls should have coeducation till they are eight in age.
2. Their education should mainly consist in manual training under the supervision of an educationist.
3. The special aptitudes of each child should be recognized in determining the kind of work he or she should do.
4. The reasons for every process should be explained when the process is being carried.
5. General knowledge should be imparted to each child as he begins to understand the things. Learning to read or write should come later.
6. The child should first be taught to draw simple geometrical figures, and when he has learnt to draw these with ease, he should be taught to write the alphabet. If this is done he will write a good hand from the very first.
7. Reading should come before writing. The letters should be treated as pictures to recognize and later on to be copied.
8. A child taught on these lines will have acquired considerable knowledge according to his capacity by the time he is eight.
9. Nothing should be taught to a child by force.
10. He should be interested in everything taught to him.

11. Education should appear to the child like play. Play is an essential part of education.
12. All education should be imparted through the mother tongue.
13. The child should be taught Hindi-Urdu as the national language, before he learns letters.
14. Religious education is indispensable and the child should get it by watching the teacher's conduct and by hearing him talk about it.
15. Nine to sixteen constitutes the second stage in the child's education.
16. It is desirable that boys and girls should have coeducation during the second stage also as far as possible.
17. Hindi children should now be taught Sanskrit, and Muslim children Arabic.
18. Manual training should be continued during the second stage. Literary education should be allotted more time according to necessity.
19. The boys during this stage should be taught their parents vocation in such a way that they will by their own choice obtain their livelihood by practicing the hereditary craft. This does not apply to the girls.
20. During this stage the child should acquire a general knowledge of the world history and geography, botany, astronomy, arithmetic, geometry and algebra.
21. Each child should now be taught to sew ant to cook.
22. Sixteen to twenty-five is the third stage, during which every young person should have an education according to his or her wishes and circumstances.
23. During the second stage (09-16) education should be self- supporting; that is, the child, all the time that he is learning, is working upon some industry, the proceeds of which will meet the expenditure of the school.
24. Production starts from the very beginning, but during the first stage it does not still catch up with the expenditure.
25. Teachers should be paid not very high salaries but only a living wage. They should be inspired by a spirit of service. It is a despicable thing to take them any Tom, Dick, or Harry as a teacher in the primary stage. All teachers should be man of character.

26. Big and expensive buildings are not necessary for educational institutions.
27. English should be taught only as one of several languages. As Hindi is the national language, English is to be used in dealing with other nations and international commerce.

As for women's education I am not sure whether it should be different from men's and when it should begin. But I am strongly of opinion that women should have the same facilities as men and even special facilities where necessary.

There should be night schools for illiterate adults. But I do not think that they must be taught the three R's; they must be helped to acquire general knowledge through lectures, etc., and if they wish, we should arrange to teach them the three R's also.

Experiments in the Ashram have convinced us of one thing, viz., that industry in general and spinning in particular should have pride of place in education, which must be largely self- supporting as well as related to and tending to the betterment of rural life.

In these experiments we have achieved the largest measure of success with the women, who have imbibed the spirit of freedom and self-confidence as no other class of women have done to my knowledge. This success is due to the Ashram atmosphere.

Women in the Ashram are not subject to any restraint which is not imposed on the men as well. They are placed on a footing of absolute equality with men in all activities. Not a single Ashram task is assigned to the women to the exclusion of the men. Cooking is attached to by both. Women are of course exempted from work which is beyond their strength; otherwise men and women work together everywhere. There is no such thing as *Purdah* or *Laj* in the Ashram. No matter form where she has come, women, as soon as she enters the Ashram, breathes the air of freedom and caste out all fear from her mind. And I believe that the Ashram observance of Brahmacharya has made a big contribution to this state of things. Adult girls live in the Ashram as virgins. We are aware that this experiment is fraught with risk but we feel that no awakening among women is possible without incurring it.

Women cannot make any progress so long as there are child marriages. All girls are supposed to be in duty bound to marry and that too before menstruation commences, and widow remarriage is not permitted. Women, therefore, when they join the Ashram, are told that these social customs are wrong and irreligious. But they are not shocked as they find the Ashram practicing what it preaches.

Not much of what is usually called education will be observed in the Ashram. Still we find that the old as well as the young, women as well as men are eager to acquire knowledge and complain that they have no time for it. This is a good sign.

Real education begins after a child has left school. One who has appreciated the value of studies is a student all his life. His knowledge must increase from day to day while he is discharging his duty in a conscientious manner. And this is well understood in the Ashram.

The superstation that no education is possible without a teacher is an obstacle in the path of educational progress. A men's real teacher is himself and nowadays there numerous aids available for self-education. A diligent person can easily acquire knowledge about many things by himself and obtain the assistance of a teacher when it is needed. Experience is the biggest of all schools. Quite a number of crafts cannot be learnt at school but only in the workshop. Knowledge of these acquired at school is often only parrot like. Other subjects can be learnt with the help of books. Therefore what adults need is not so much a school as a thirst for knowledge, diligence and self-confidence?

The education of children is primarily a duty to be discharged by the parents. Therefore the creation of a vital educational atmosphere is more important than the foundation of numerous schools. When once this atmosphere has been established on a firm footing the schools will come in the course. *(History of the Satyagraha Ashram, 11 July 1932 (CW 50, PP. 232-36))*

LESSONS FROM EXPERIMENTS IN EDUCATION BY GANDHI IN SOUTH AFRICA AND INDIA

The view and philosophy of Gandhis are the result of his experiments and his studies (ancient as well as modern).

The narrative of Gandhis educational experiments and the results of these experiments in India begin in the year 1915 when Gandhiji paid a visit to Shantiniketan. It is not much known that "The phoenix" family had been assigned separate quarters at Shantiniketan. Thus Shantiniketan can be said to be a confluence of two types of educational experiments: phoenix-development experiments and the experiments by Gurudeva Rabindranath Tagore.

Gandhiji initiated "self-help" in running the kitchen or the "kitchen revolution". The teachers and students of phoenix, under the guidance of Gandhiji, decided to dispense with the paid cooks and to cook their food themselves. The Shantiniketan students also started a kitchen for themselves. The experiment worked well in the beginning, but it was dropped after some time. According to Gandhiji, Shantiniketan lost nothing by having conducted the experiment for a brief interval, and some of the experiences gained could not but be of help to the teachers. Gurudeva comment was "the experiment contains the key to Swaraj".

There were certain important sayings with which Gandhi used to explain his educational policy. As a part of experiments in truth and experiments in education, Gandhi had developed certain beliefs. In South Africa, in his early years of life gandhis had very seriously changed from the simplest to the costliest. He undertook and brought out certain changes. These changes were more internal than external.

As a part of assigning an importance to the virtues such as self-reliance, self-dependence, Gandhiji did not insist that the work should be of cleaning the closets done by the servants in the house. This proved a good training for the children and none of Gandhi's sons and other children developed aversion for scavengers work; they got a good grounding in sanitation. One of the underlying or foundational tenets of Gandhi's educational approach is that the children inherit the qualities of the parents. The educational experiments on Tolstoy Farm and Phoenix settlements were necessitated by the growth of these Ashrams. There was an increase in the demand for funds which were needed in more and more quantities.

Gandhi's philosophy of education was the result of his theoretical studies, his meditation and contemplation and his experiments in the "laboratory" of life. As it has been said earlier also, his all experiments, including those relating education were comprehensive, deep, well thought out. These experiments has been conducted in South Africa and India, they related to education of children and households, they were about curriculum, they were conducted and Tolstoy Farm and Phoenix settlement or Phoenix Ashram.

As a part of his experiments, Gandhiji realized the value of manual labour and spiritual training.

Gandhiji educational experiments were partly conducted at Shantiniketan, the fact which is not widely known to the people. The Ashrams, other institutions, universities and colleges where he conducted educational experiments were: Satyagraha Ashram at Kochrab, National Gujarati school, the National Education, National Higher Education, Gujarat Vidyapith, Village Schools, Nayee Taleem, Crafts, etc.

There is another important matter from which Gandhiji has drawn an important lesson. The question is whether we should treat students unequally, differently for one reason or other? Gandhiji learnt a lesson at Tolstoy Farm. At this Ashram, Gandhis three children also studied. When it was suggested that Gandhiji should keep his boys separately, Gandhiji rejected the suggestion saying that if good children are taught together with bad ones, they will lose nothing provided experiment is conducted under the watchful care of their parents and guardians.

In Gandhi's own words,'… the ultimate result of my experiments is in the womb of the future.' If one is allowed to hazard an assessment here, we may say that the thinking and /or behaviour and the whole life of the eldest son of Gandhiji (Hari) supports the view that it is the Gandian thinking, Gandian vision which will have the test of time.

Gandhi's approach was religious, he asked students to be aware of and familiar with their scriptures, and they must be acquainted with elements of their own religion. Does it mean that Gandhiji practiced secularism in his educational experiments? Basically, his approach to everything and experiences was religious or spiritual.

Gandhiji experiments and experiences in South Africa strengthened his conviction that spiritual training was a thing by itself. The training of the spirit of the young enabled one to work towards the knowledge of God and self-realization, and all that training without culture of the spirit was of no use, and it may even harm education.

Agriculture as a basic craft

"Some people ask me why Agriculture could not be a basic craft. The answer is that it has not the educational potentialities of spinning. It cannot, for example, develop deftness as in spinning. The function of Nayee Taleem is not merely to teach an occupation, but through it to develop the whole men."

"But through I do not begin with agriculture, it is bound to come in ultimately. For, the field of New Education is comprehensive. The pupils and teachers of the school of my conception will together have to make provision for all they need. A teacher of Nayee Taleem will have to be a first-class craftsman. All the children of the village will be themselves drawn to the school. In this way, education would become free and universal. "

"Today, the condition of India is that Vegetables grown in a Village are not available for the use of the villagers themselves. The villagers of Travancore cannot use the coconuts that are grown there. They are collected at one place and sent to the towns. This anomaly will disappear where basic schools come into existence. Again, today we will cultivate food crops which they themselves need." *(Harijan, 09 November 1947)*

IDEALISM, THE FOUNDATION OF GANDIAN THOUGHTS

Indian philosophy and religious thoughts constitute the background of the idealist framework of Ghandi in his attitudes towards education. In Gandhi we find an educational eclecticism of a characteristic type in which idealism, naturalism and pragmatism have found a place. Gandhi's aim was not to develop a professed school or tenet of philosophy. He was responding, in his own characteristics manner, to the educational needs of his time and he attempted at the same time to evolve a workable system to meet the need and to develop a rationale necessary for such a system. Idealism became the very foundation of the Gandian System of education into which other tenets of thoughts have also found their way.

Will Durant says, "Gandhi is above all an idealist, not realist; he leaps far ahead in the moral consciousness of humanity". Gandhi's attempt was not merely to discover or propose passing and temporary solutions to problems of education; instead he tried to cross the limits of traditional thinking and to education to permanent and lasting values and principles through his idealistic thoughts. Bhatia says, "Ghandi was an idealist to the core. He has stressed the dignity of man and the significance of value in life like an idealistic thinker". He possessed the pervasiveness, the depth of vision and the comprehensiveness of an idealist in his attitude towards education.

As an idealist Gandhi's depth of vision in education and in life takes him to ultimate values. No educationist in history dealing with practical problems of gigantic dimensions could so daringly fix his feet so well in God and spiritual values and permeate the entire scheme of education with these values. Luis Fischer says "Ghandi faced each morning's issues in the light of eternal and universal values". He was not the least embarrassed to defend his moral and spiritual foundations in a more materialistic world of twentieth century which wanted education nothing to do with the world of religion and spirituality. For Ghandi the values related to the ultimate goals of education are absolute and unchanging. Man is expected to understand, accept and live these values to the best of his ability. Man's conscience. Is to be shaped accordingly, and not to shape the values to the satisfaction of the individual's relative conscience. Donald Harrington remarks, "All the questions that were asked he answered easily and spontaneously as from an inexhaustible wealth of spiritual assurance". Ghandi wanted education to develop this spiritual assurance by shaping in individual's conscience in the practice of the values related to the ultimate goals of life and education.

Gandian idealism and educational practices

It is fundamental to idealism that the human mind is educated to generate experiences in the process of leading the mind to greater maturity and perfection is an important term in the context of educational idealism. The human mind is created to arrive at a level of perfection envisaged or planned by its creator. The duty of education is to explore the possibilities of enhancing the individual's perfection and provide the conditions necessary for the realisation of it. When Gandhi introduced the craft system it was designed to educate "the whole man: mind, body and soul." The craft he thought would enable the highest form of education of the mind and the soul. Ghandi says, "Man is not sheer intellect, animal body, heart or soul. To create a whole and integral man a suitable and perfect integration of these is required. This exactly is the essence of education". He calls craft-centered education as "the education of the brain by the use of the hands." The craft puts the individual's mind into productive work and sets a movement in the line of the idealistic perfection.

Gandhi saw the craft as the very centre of early education around which other subjects and experiences were to be provided. For Gandhi craft was "the meeting point of both physical and social environment represented by such subjects as general sciences, social sciences, and creative and expressional arts." Like a true idealist Gandhi attaches the greatest spiritual point, again, of experience that would arise from the handicraft the individual raises his mind in a variety of ways to the contemplation of the divine values permeating life's activities. Gandian education provides opportunities of physical and intellectual nature for developing experiences of this kind that would in turn lead to mind in steps to the idealistic perfection in truth, love and beauty. The whole education becomes a chain of such experiences towards the perfection of the individual's character.

Idealistic education puts increasing stress on the dignity of the human personality with reference to the educational experiences that are provided. Gandhi writes, "If teachers aim at developing the discriminative powers of the boys and girls under them, they will continually foster their reasoning capacity and enable them to think for themselves". The dignity of personality in the Gandhian sense consists primarily in being able to think for oneself and become physically, emotionally and spiritually independent. Chester

Bowles writes, "He conceived of sevagram as a place where peace is natural and human dignity is fully recognized. Above all human labour has become dignified and creative". Gandhi was throughout conscious of this dignity of the human individual. He believed as he professed that the logical finale of this dignity of human being lies in his communion with society through service through and love of neighbor, and in his communion with god in prayer.

Gandhi exhorts students to be independent in their thinking, and enhance the powers of the human soul. This is thought of as the foundation of the freedom that Gandhi envisages. Education should do everything at its disposal to secure this freedom for the individual by providing, again, the necessary experiences. Ghandi writes, "Experience of the soul is the richest and the only one that helps our development". Gandhi proposes fearlessness to be the care corner-stone of the freedom of mind that the student should secure for himself. Gandhi said to students, "we live in constant fear. We fear spiritual dependency just as we fear the worldly power and authority ...... we fear worldly forces. By doing that we causing harm to ourselves and to them...". Gandhi made it very clear that we should have absolutely no fear other than the fear of God. This fearlessness he proposes to be the foundation of the freedom of spirit, dignity of human personality and the integrity of the mind that education should nurture in the individual.

Gandhi constantly referred back to the ancient Vedic education and the ashram type of education that prevailed in the *Gurukula*. The *gurukula* education was highly teacher centered in theory and practice. The dignity, the honour, the respect and the authority that the teacher or the *guru* commanded contributed to the success of the great spiritual basis that Vedic education established and the character formation that was achieved by the students. That was exactly the western idealistic position too. Traditional western idealism was highly teacher-centered rather than child or life-centered. Just as the idealist wants "fine roses" from the garden of education Gandhi is not content with anything less than the finest roses of truth, love and ahimsa. Like any true idealist Gandhi is not satisfied with anything less than God himself as supreme perfection in truth and love. The teacher's authority becomes a means, a powerful means in the realisation of this supreme perfection in students.

Genuine freedom for Gandhi came from self-discipline John Holmes remarks, "Gandhi had a disciplined process of putting his soul to work, with results that were patent to all, but none the less hard to understand". This self-discipline that the exercised in every detail of his life has everything to do with his spiritual orientations and proved to be one of the most powerful weapons in the practice of truth and ahimsa. Albert Einstein wrote. "Gandhi's work on behalf of India's liberation is the living testimony to the fact that man's will, sustained by an indomitable conviction, and is more powerful than material forces that seem unsurmountable". Gandhi's idealistic vision of life and education enabled him to present to education a world of "high thinking and simple living" adequate for a country like India.

The following are the chief characteristics of idealism of Gandhiji.

1. **Concept of education-** Gandhiji summed up his ideas on education in these words. "By education I mean an all-round drawing out of the best in child and man-body, mind and spirit."
2. **Education for character Development-** Gandhiji said, "The end of all knowledge must be building up character. What is education without character and what is character without elementary personal purity?"
3. **Role of the Teacher in the spiritual and moral training of the students-** Gandhiji observed, just as physical training was to be imparted through physical exercise, even so the training of the spirit entirely depended on the life and character of the teacher.
4. **An ideal Teacher-** Gandhiji said, "The teacher is ideal who teaches one thing with the lips and carries another in his heart."
5. **Freedom but under discipline-** Gandhiji emphatically said, "The highest form of freedom carries with it the greatest measures of discipline and humility. Freedom that comes from discipline and humility cannot be denied, unbridled license is a sign of vulgarity injurious alike to self and one's neighbors."

GANDHIJIS PRAGMATISM IN EDUCATION

Gandhiji emphasized activity curriculum. Like all pragmatists he advocated learning by experience and learning by activity. Learning by experience was the chief force his methods of teaching which can be seen as follows-

1. **Experimental Approach-** Like other pragmatist. Gandhiji believes in an experimental approach towards life. He calls his biography as 'My experiments with truth'. He talks of two types of truth- the relative truth

and the absolute truth. According to his view point, the conception of relative truth is always subjected to experimentation and modification. The absolute truth of God is final.

2. **Self-knowledge Acquire-** In the field of education, Gandhiji advocates with the pragmatist that the child should acquire knowledge himself. This will help him to solve his future situations in later life.

3. **Project Method-** The project method of the pragmatist and the basic schemes of Mahatma Gandhi have many common points. Both these methods are based on the principle activity and interests.

4. **Specialized activity-** The project method is based on some specialized activity. It means that the activity is to be in a social setting. In the same way the basic craft is chosen keeping in the view that the craft of the community. Hence, it will be a socialized activity and will bring forth relationship with the community as well.

GANDHIS NATURALISM IN EDUCATION

Gandhiji introduced several elements of naturalism in education and this becomes clear from the following-

1. **Craft work as natural meeting of all subjects**- craft work is the meeting point of all

2. **Subjects.** The correlated teaching arouses greater interest and enthusiasm because it gives teaching and learning a relevance born of practical and living purposes and need. Craft work done under proper conditions not only makes the acquisition of much related knowledge more concrete and realistic but also adds a powerful contribution to the development of personality and character and instills respects and love for all society useful work.

3. **Medium of Instruction**- Gandhiji wrote, " Our language is the reflection of ourselves and if you tell me that our language are too poor to express the best thought, I say that the sooner we are wiped out of existence the better for us." About foreign medium he observed, "The foreign medium had made our children practically foreigners in their own land".

4. **Freedom for the child-** Like the naturalists he advocates freedom for the child. "if the children are to find themselves, they must be allowed a sufficient degree of freedom; if they are to develop their powers to the fullest, they must be prepared to accept the appropriate discipline and training."

5. **Educational in Natural surroundings-** Gandhiji greatly stressed the importance of educating the child in natural surroundings. He expects "the teachers to educate village children in their villages so as to draw out all their faculties through some handicrafts."

6. **Gandhian scheme: An Assessment**

One of the discussions that have surfaced in an assessment of Gandhi has centered round the question: Is Gandhi an idealist, a naturalist or a pragmatist educator? In his emphasis on an ideal society- a Ramarajya, he is an idealist. In his belief that education is for the liberation of the mind, it is for self-realisation through social service, his conception of the child as a spark of the divine etc; he is an idealist. As he wrote in two issues of young India: "I believe in the absolute oneness of God (advaita) and therefore, of humanity. What through us may have many bodies? We have but one soul. The rays of the sun are many through refraction. But they have the same source?" again, "My creed is service of God, and therefore, of humanity." In his educational settings, in natural surroundings, Ashram-life, gurukula type of education etc; he was a naturalist. His activity-centered curriculum also was in line with naturalistic sensory education. He was against text-book education.

He was an experimentalist to the core, and hence a pragmatist. He believed in 'learning by doing' methods of teaching. He was always open-minded and did not claim any finality in truth. He practiced first and then preached it. In this sense, he was a pragmatist. As Dr. R. S. Mani has observed: "However, much his experiments may be characterized by qualities of accuracy, foresight and minuteness, he does not claim his results to be infallible. Whatever appeared to be absolutely correct for him, seemed for the time being to be final." Winding up the discussion, M.S.

patel considers that Gandhi was three-in-one idealist, a naturalist and a pragmatist. As he puts it:

"The real greatness of Gandhiji as an educationist consists in the fact that the dominant tendencies of naturalism, idealism and pragmatist are not separate and independent in his philosophy, but they are fused into a unity, giving rise to a theory of education which would suit the needs of the day and satisfy the loftiest aspirations of the human soul." This and not the scheme of basic education is his greatest achievement.

Chapter 3
Gandhis Nai Talim (Basic Education) part II

GANDHIAN EDUCATION AT VARIOUS STAGES

Early childhood education

Education children should be normally the easiest of things, but somehow it has become, or been made, the most difficult. Experience shows that the children are always learning one thing or another whether we notice it or not and whether what they learn is good or bad. This may seem strange to some readers. But if we would consider carefully-who is a child; what is education and who is best qualified to teach the children? - The observation made above would not seem strange and might even appear quite correct.

By children we mean young boys and girls not more than 10 years of age. Then education does not mean simply the knowledge of letters-the capacity to read and write. The knowledge of letters is only one of the means of education. Really speaking, education consists in learning to use in the right way all one's sense-organs, including the mind. In other words, the child should know how to use his organs of action such as hands and feet, etc. as also his organs of knowledge such as the nose, the eyes, etc. a boy who knows that he should not use his hands in stealing things or killing flies or beating the younger brothers, sisters and playmates has already made a good beginning on his way to education.

The same may be said of the boy who understands the need for keeping his teeth, tongue, ears, eyes, nails, etc. clean and does so. A boy who does not indulge in pranks while eating or drinking, who has learnt to eat and drink in a right manner whether alone or in company, who knows the distinction between wholesome and unwholesome food and chooses the former, who does not overeat, who does not ask for every new thing that he sees and who, when he asks for it and does not get it, remains quite, may he said to have progressed quite a great deal in his education.

Whose pronunciation is good, who can tell the history and geography of his region- even though he may not know these terms,- who knows what is meant by the motherland, he has traversed a fairly good distance on the read to education. Similarly with him who has learnt to distinguish between truth and untruth, between good and evil and who invariably chooses what is true and good, there is no need to further elaborate the point. The readers can fill in the pictures themselves. Only I should make one thing clear. There is no need of the knowledge of reading and writing in order to learn the things I have spoken of above. To make the boys to learn the alphabet is to put an undue burden on their young minds and to misuse their eyes and hands. A rightly educated boy gets to learn reading and writing almost without any effort and, what is more, gladly at the proper time. At the present time, however, this thing becomes a heavy burden upon him.

Much of the valuable time which could be put to better us gets to waste and in the end, instead of producing shapely letters or acquiring pronunciation, all that they succeed in doing is to produce misshapen letters and cultivate a bad handwriting. As for reading, they read much which had better been left unread and read it indifferently without any sense of pronunciation. To call it education is to abuse that august term. The boy must first get elementary knowledge before learning to read and write. If this is done our poor country would be saved from much unnecessary expense incurred on various readers and children's books and many other evils. If children's readers are at all thought necessary they should be written for use by the teachers and not for boys of my conception. But for our drifting with the current vogue this thing should be as clear to us as daylight.

The boys can get the education I have spoken of only at home and that too only through the mother. In a way, all boys do get some sort of an education from the mother. But seeing that the home has disintegrated, so to say, and seeing that most parents are not equal to the task. The boys should be placed in surroundings where they will get the same atmosphere as they do at home. Since of all persons the mother is the most competent to undertake the duty of educating the children, this particular task should be entrusted only to women. As a rule men are far behind women in respect of love and patience. If this is true the question of the education of children cannot be solved unless efforts are made simultaneously to solve the women's education. And I have no hesitation in saying that as long as we do not have real mother-teachers who can successfully impart true education to our children they will remain uneducated even though they may be going to schools.

Let me now set forth in brief an outline of the children's education. Suppose that a mother-teacher is entrusted with five children. These children have no training in manners. They do not speak distinctly. They do not know how to walk or even to sit in the right manner. The nose, eyes, ears, and nails are dirty. Asked to sit, they stretch out their legs and when they speak, they mumble. They have no knowledge of directions. The clothes are putting in their mouths. The border of the cap on the head has turned black and sticky and it gives out a foul odour. Now the teacher in question can train them only if she has the heart of a mother. The first lesson she has to give them would be that of cleanliness. She will drench them with her love and amuse them in various ways as only mothers know how to do and as did Kaushalya her Rama and thus she will bind them to her with the ties of love and so will be in a position to secure from them willing compliance to all that she wants. She will know no rest until these boys have learnt to keep neat and tidy, until their teeth, ears, hands and feet are clean, until they learn to take care of their clothes and have improved their pronunciation. Having accomplished this she will first teach them *Ramanama*-the name of Lord God. He has many names and it does not matter by which name he is called.

The next in order after *dharma* is *artha*, i.e., the temporal knowledge. So she will now set out to teach them arithmetic. She will get them to learn the multiplication tables and teach them addition and subtraction- as much of it as can be managed orally. The boys must know the place where they live, so she will tell them of the rivers and rivulets, hills, buildings of interest, etc. and in the process give them the knowledge of directions. She will improve her own knowledge for the sake of the children. History and geography are not to be treated as separate subjects in this method. Both will be taught by way of stories. She will not however be content with this. A Hindu mother will recite Sanskrit verses to her children from their infancy, so that they get used to the pronunciation of Sanskrit words. She will get them to learn Sanskrit verses in praise of God. A patriotic mother will of course teach them Hindi too.

She next in therefore converse with them in Hindi. She will read out to them selected passages from Hindi books and thus make them bilingual. She will not teach them the alphabet yet, but she will certainly give them the brush, she will get them to trace the geometrical figures-to draw straight lines and circles. A boy who cannot draw a flower or a water-jug or a triangle cannot be said to be educated, again, she will not but introduce them to good music. She will not tolerate the children being unable to sing in unison the national song or hymns, etc. she will teach them to sing to the accompaniment of time. If possible, she will give them *ektara*, or *jhanjih*. To make them physically fir she will get them to do physical exercises, to practice running and jumping. Then, the boys should also be taught the love of service and various skills. She will therefore teach them spinning with all the ancillary processes beginning from the picking of cotton pods. And these boys will willingly spin for at least half an hour every day.

Most of the textbooks which we have today are useless for this purpose. The mother-teacher therefore will find out or produce new ones and her love for the children will help her in this task. Every village has its own history and geography; naturally it will have its own history-book and geography-book. The arithmetical exercises too will be new. The mother-teacher will prepare the lessons she wants to teach the children herself every day, she will produce new sums and will always have many new things to say to the boys- which she will note down in her notebook when she prepares the lesson. Her lesson in the class will thus be not a mechanical performance but something lively and creative.

The syllabus will vary according to the progress of the children. It should therefore be drawn up after every three months. The children constituting the class come them different homes-each has his own different background of nurture. We cannot therefore have the same syllabus for all of them. At times it may be necessary even to induce them to unlearn what they have learnt. For example, if a six or seven year old child has learnt to trace letters in a slovenly way or has picked up the habit of reading without trying to understand what he reads, the mother-teacher will see that he unlearns all that. She must cast out the illusion that the child can acquire knowledge only through reading. It is easy enough to understand that even one who never had any training in reading can be wise.

I have not used the word teacher in this article; I have throughout used the word 'mother-teacher' in its place. Because the teacher must really be a mother to the children she teaches. One who cannot take the place of a mother cannot be a teacher. The child should never feel that he is being taught. Let her simply keep her eye upon him and guide him. A child who spends six hours in the school will possibly be wasting his time while the former will be learning something or the other all the time in terms of real education.

It is likely that we may not get good women-teachers in the existing conditions. That being so we may make use of men for the purpose. In that case these men-teachers will have to fill the place of the mother. But eventually it is the mother who will have to undertake the task. But if it I am right any mother the children can easily prepare herself for it. And she can also prepare the children at the same time that she is preparing herself. *(Navajivan, 2 June 1929 (CW 41, PP.5-9))*

Nursery Education

I saw the work done by teachers trained under Madame Montessori, and carefully observed the working of the Nursery School. Of course the things were foreign and the poor teacher had not digested what she had been taught. What to speak of the children? They could not even observe normal discipline. I am not criticizing anyone. I have given the gist of my experience just for your information. Imbibe whatever you find useful and discard the rest. The conclusion I have drawn from this experience is that we shall be able to propagate scientific knowledge of child education only when our teachers are competent. They should have the will to become one with children. I am afraid I am not saying anything new in this. These things are certainly not beyond your range of experience but since I have come to know you and also love you I hope you will not find fault with me for saying the things you already know. *(Letter to Tarabehn Modak, 16 October 1945 (CW 81, P.364))*

Primary Education

After a great deal of reflection and experimentation I have come to the conclusion that primary education should be given for at least a year without books and even after that the use of books should be restricted to the minimum.

If books are introduced from the very start and the children made to master the alphabet, the development of their various abilities are arrested and their intelligence stunted, although this is the time when it should grow rapidly. A child begins to learn immediately after its birth, but mostly through the eyes and ears or though the senses. And, as soon as he has learnt to speak, i.e., to imitate the sound of words, he begins rapidly to acquire the use of language. Naturally he picks up the same language as that of his parents. If the parents have taste and refinement, he also develops those qualities. He pronounces the words correctly and copies their good manners and conduct. This is his real education. And if our culture and traditions had not fallen apart, children would still be receiving the best kind of education in their homes.

But looking at the deplorable conditions in which we are living at present this cannot be and there is no alternative save to send our boys to schools. But if the child has to go to a school, we must see that it looks like a home to him and the teachers like parents, and the education provided should be such as would be provided in a cultural home. This means that all preliminary teaching should be oral. A child educated in this way would learn in a year ten times more than the boy taught in the other way, i.e., through the alphabet.

Oral teaching would enable the children to know the usual rudiments of history and geography much in the same way as they get to know stories, quite easily, in the very first year. They would commit to memory a fairly good number of poems; and they would learn the counting of numbers almost automatically without any effort. And because they would not be subjected to the burden of recognizing and learning the alphabet, the growth of their minds would not be stopped and their eyes would not be misused.

They would use their hands not in tracing different letters-a practice which spoils their handwriting for good-but in drawing the figures of geometry and simple pictures. This would be good preliminary training for the hand, as it would develop both coordination and skill.

And if we want to provide education to the crores of children of Gujarat and of India, this is the only way in which primary education should be imparted to them.

Under the conditions existing in the country it is impossible to give books to children. I admit that if it is necessary to give books to children in the primary stage also, then attempts must be made to do so whatever the expenditure, but if they are considered unnecessary and even harmful then this plea for stopping the use of books in the initial years. The idea should be given a fair trial. A thing which is unnecessary from the moral point of view is always found to be impermissible also from the practical point of view. In an ideal civilization morality and what is called practical policy are not two contradictory things.

Lastly, it is clear that the present group of teachers cannot be expected to give effect to the scheme of education presented here. They may manage to teach the boys the alphabet and also simple arithmetic. But they themselves are ignorant of the type of knowledge which, according to the scheme I have sketched, should be made available to how can they help the boys to from the habit of correct speech? (Navajivan, 13 May 1928 *(Problem of Education, PP.147-49))*

Secondary Education

A system of education has to be so conceived as to be an instrument of protection of the freedom of a nation.

Hence, we must make our experiments in education. It may well be that in the course of these experiments we get to know the experiences which Europe has had; but we should never give credence to the idea that everything European is good, or that what is good for Europe under the conditions obtaining there will also be good for us here in India. Granting that this line of reasoning is correct, one of the conclusions it leads us to is that we should evaluate what goes on in the Government schools critically. Knowing as we do that Government education is detrimental to Swaraj and destructive of our civilization, we are likely to get at the right solution for us if we do just the opposite of what is done in the Government schools. Let us now study examples:

There, the medium of education in English. We should know from this that it should never be permitted in national education.

There, they have big expensive buildings. We should know that this is undesirable. The buildings' of our school should be simple-as befit the poor.

There, they concentrate on mere literacy and the study of language and literature and neglect the indigenous crafts. Evidently this is not right.

There they leave out the teaching of religion-I mean the basic principles common to all religious and not any particular creeds. We know that this has the effect of nullifying the good that the rest of the education might ordinarily do to students. History, as taught in Government schools, if not wholly untrue, is presented essentially from the point of view of the British Government. German, French and American historians would treat and interpret the same material in a different way. Even recent events, as for example, the Punjab Massacre is presented by Government writers in one way and by nationalist writers in quite another light.

Economics, as taught in Government schools, approves of the policies of the Government, while we look at them from a totally different point of view.

While in Government primary schools, the teachers are appointed without any consideration of their character, in our schools they must be men of the highest character. The former have only the minimum qualifications for the work they are expected to do and are paid the lowest salaries. The latter, on other hand, should be highly qualified men and though they will also be paid low salaries, the reason would be their selflessness and not their helplessness.

This, I think, should give you some idea of the type of education which should be given in our city schools.

Our students should be men who will work for the stabilization and revitalization of our rural civilization. They would study the needs of the villagers, try to remove the defects they may discover in them and train their children to become good farmers and good villagers and not to be lured by the dazzle of the cities. Thus, as long as we do not set about to make a radical changes in the form and content of the education now going on in the cities, we cannot fulfill one of the important aims of the Vidyapith. Take only one example: we are running three institutions in Ahmadabad-the Mahvidyalaya or the college, the New Gujarati Pathashala, and the Vinaya Mandir or the secondary school. We have the right to run these institutions only if we mean to try to make good villagers of the students studying in them. They should have a thorough knowledge of village life and develop a love for it. Eventually, those of them who pass out of the Mahavidyalaya or the Vinaya Mandir, after having completed their studies, should spread out in the villages and immerse themselves in the service of the people there. *(Navajivan, 20 May 1928 (CW 36, PP. 327-29))*

College education

I would revolutionize college education and relate it to national necessities. There would be degree for mechanical and other engineers. They would be attached to the different industries which should pay for the training of the graduates they need. Thus the Tatas would be expected to run a college for training engineers under the supervision of the state, the mill associations would run among a college for training graduates whom they need.

Similarly for the other industries that may be named. Commerce will have its college. There remain arts, medicine and agriculture. Several private arts colleges are today self-supporting. The state would, therefore, cease to run its own. Medical colleges would be attached to certified hospitals. As they are popular among moneyed men they may be expected by voluntary contributions to support medical colleges. And agriculture colleges to be worthy of the name must be self-supporting. I have a painful experience of some agricultural graduates. Their knowledge is superficial. They lack pratical experiences. But if they had their apprenticeship on farms which are self-sustained and answer the requirements of the country, they would not have to gain experiences after getting their degrees and at the expense of their employers. *(Harijan, 31 July 1937 (CW 65, P. 451))*

State universities

Higher education should be left to private enterprise and for meeting national requirements whether in the various industries, technical arts, belles-letters or fine arts.

The state universities should be purely examining bodies, self-supporting through the fees charged for examinations.

Universities will look after the whole of the field of education and will prepare and approve courses of studies in the various departments of education. No private school should be run without the previous sanction of the respective universities. University charters should be given liberally to anybody of persons of proved worth and integrity, it being always understood that the universities will not cost the state anything except that it will bear the cost of running a Central Educational Department.

The foregoing scheme does not achieve the state from running such seminaries as may be required for supplying State needs. *(Harijan, 2 October 1937)*

Reorientation of University Education

Gandhiji remarked at the conference of Education Ministers in Poona that what he had said about adult education applied to university education. It must be originally related to the Indian scene. It must therefore be an extension and continuation of the Basic Education Course. That was the central point. If they did not see eye to eye with him on that point, he was afraid they would have little use for his advice. If, on the other hand, they agreed with him that the present University education did not fit them for independence but only enslaved them, they would be as impatient as he was to completely overhaul and scrap that system and remodel it on new lines consonant with the national requirement.

Today the youth educated in our universities either after the Government jobs or fell into devious ways and sought outlet for their frustration by fomenting unrest. They were not even ashamed to beg or sponge upon others. Such was their sad plight. The aim of University education should be to turn out true servants of the people, who would live and die for the country's freedom. He was therefore of opinion that university education should be considered and brought into line with 'Basic Education, by taking in teachers from the Talimi Sangh. *(Harijan, 25 August 1946)*

WOMEN EDUCATION AND COEDUCATION:

Mahatma Gandhi viewed women illiteracy as no better than a curse and strongly vouched for its promotion among women. (Garai, 2015). Women's mental capacity is equal to men and therefore she has equal right to have an education (Anuradha, 2016). But Mahatma Gandhi's view on women education is based on family ideals. He believed that man is superlative in the extra-mural activities and that woman is supreme in intra-mural activities. Therefore, education provided to both men and women should be according to their pre-ordained stations in life (Nandela).

Equality of rights for women

We shall accept equality of rights for women, but I think their education should differ from men's as their nature and functions do. In progressive countries, women receive the very highest education but, after it is over, they do not have to perform the same duties as men and in our country women have never to compete with men for a livelihood. (Prajabandhu, 27 February 1916 (CW 13, P. 246) (Translated from Gujarati))

Educated Women's Role

The women whom this message reaches are likely to have had some measure of education. I wish, therefore, to consider one thing. What should educated women do for their illiterate sisters? This is a very important issue. Beyond question, if women choose... they can attain a far greater measure of success in this field than men can ever do. At present, we do not find many women taking to this work. That is, I believe, not their fault but that of their education. The first thing, therefore, which educated women must do, is to try and see that their sisters do not fell a victim to it. Modern Education fails utterly to prepare women for their distinctive role; this is not questioned by anyone. I do not wish here to examine the shortcomings of modern education or to bother you with the question how they may be overcome. All that I desire is that educated women should make this question their own and that those of them with some experience should dedicate their all to rouse Gujarat over it and focus attention on the right lines of reform.

Educated women have no contact with those not educated; often, they don't welcome such contacts. This disease must be cured. It is necessary that educated women are made conscious of their most obvious duty. Men also are not free from faults of this kind, but women need not follow in their footsteps. They have the power, denied to men, of creating new ideals and translating them into action. By comparison, men is thoughtless, impatient and given to the pursuit of novelty. *(Gujarati, 2 November 1917 (CW 14, PP. 86-87)*

Men versus women's Education

The education of women is as faulty as that of men. They have not given any thought to the relations obtaining between men and women, or to the place women occupies in Indian society.

It may be admitted that for the most part preliminary teaching of both boys and girls would be much the same. Barring that, there is great dissimilarity. There is need for similar distinction between the education of males and females as has been made between them by Mother Nature herself. True, they are equals. But there is a difference in the work they are ordained to do. It is women's right to rule inside the home. Men are master outside it. Man is the earner of livelihood, women saves and spends. Women bring up children. She is their mother. She is responsible for building up their character. She is their educator, and hence the *mother of the race*. Man is not, in that sense, *the father of the race*. After a certain age a father ceases to influence his son, but not so the mother. The son, even after attaining manhood, behaves like a child in the presence of his mother. He cannot, however, do this with his father.

If this arrangement is considered natural and right a women should not have to earn her living. A society in which women have to work as telegram clerks, typists or compositors is, I think, not well-organized. It is a symptom of moral and economic bankruptcy and is an indication that they, i.e., the people belonging to that society, have begun to live on their capital. Hence, just as it is wrong to keep women in ignorance and under suppression on the one hand, it is wrong, on the other hand, to entrust them with the work which is ordinarily done by men, for this is a sign of weakness and is tantamount to oppression.

Therefore, after a certain age, there must be arrangements to provide women with a kind of education different to that of men. Women should be taught the management of the home, the things they should or should not do during pregnancy, and the nursing and care of children. It is difficult to make up suitable arrangements for providing such teaching as the idea is a new one. The right course under the circumstances would be to constitute a committee of enlightened and experienced men and women of good character who would then explore the problem, come to the right decision, and produce a suitable plan for the purpose. This committee should find out how best to impart the necessary education girls after they have completed the period of childhood and enter on that of womanhood. But, unfortunately, there are a large number of girls in our country who get married even while they are in their childhood. Besides, the number goes on increasing. And once they are married, they just disappear from social life. I have expressed my views about them fully in my foreword contributed to the first book of the *"Bhagini Pustak-mala"* series. I reproduced them here:

"We cannot achieve the education of women merely by educating girls. Claimed by the monster of child-marriage, thousands of girls disappear from view at the early age of twelve. From girls they change into house-wives at one stroke. As long as this wicked custom continues, the only alternative is that men must learn to act as teachers to women. A great many of our hopes in regard to the education of women rest on how men discharge their duty in this respect. Women must cease to be our servants and objects of enjoyment as they are at present, and become, instead, our lift-companions, equal partners in the battle of life, shares in our happiness and unhappiness. All our efforts seem utterly futile as long as this is not accomplished. There are some men who regard their women as beasts. For this sad state some of the Sanskrit sayings and the following well-known Doha of Tulsidas may be held responsible. Tulsidas says at one place in his Ramayana: "The drum, the food, the Shudra and the Women-all these are fit objects to beat." I hold Tulasidasji in high esteem, but my worship is not blind. Either this couplet is an interpolation, or, if it is his, he must have written it without thought-as reflecting the prevailing views of the then society. As to the saying in Sanskrit, people seem to be laboring under the impression that every shloka written is, as it were, a scriptural precept. We must fight this impression and eradicate from its very root the custom of regarding women as inferior beings. On the other hand, blinded by passion many among us adore women and decorate them with ornaments just as we decorate idols. We must keep away from this evil also. Our ultimate goal, *however, will not be achieved until our women become to us what Parvati was to Mahadeva, Sita to Rama, Damayanti to Nala. Then, they participate in our discussions, argue things with us on an equal basis, understand through their wonderful insight born of sympathy, be partners in our fight for resolving them and become for us, when we need it, he givers of the most soothing peace. This goal cannot be achieved merely by starting girl's schools. As long as we have around our necks the noose of child marriage, men must be the teachers of their womenfolk. And this education which men will give to women will not be merely literacy; it will be extended to cover social reform and politics. Literacy must be only a preliminary to the teaching of the other subjects mentioned above. These may be taught even without it. A man who undertakes to teach his wife in this manner will have to change his attitude towards her. A man will himself be a student with his wife and will observe complete celibacy in his relation with her until she attains maturity. In no case will he subject a girl of twelve to fifteen years of age to the agony of bearing children to him. One ought to shudder at the very thought of it. If this is done we will not be crushed under the weight of inertia as we are at present.*

"Classes are being started for married women and lecturers arranged for them. All this is good as far as it goes. Those who are engaged in this work are sacrificing their time and energy for a good cause. This is quite creditable. But simultaneously men must also undertake to discharge the duty indicated above, because in its absence all these efforts will not bear much result. On deeper reflection, I am sure that what I have said is self-evident." (Speech at Second Gujarat Educational Conference, 20 October 1917 (CW 14, PP. 31-33))

Women, like Man, Needs Education

Though much good and useful work can be done without knowledge of reading and writing, yet I believe that such knowledge is necessary, for one can hardly do without it these days. Reading of good books develops the intellect and that, in its turn, increases our capacity for service to our people and our country. I do not over-estimate the value of this knowledge, but I should like to give it its due place in the scheme of things. I have pointed out on several occasions that lack of education among women should not be made the reason for men to deprive them of their due human rights.

But proper education is essential in order that they may use those rights well, adorn them and spread them amongst our masses. Without proper education and the knowledge acquired through such education, millions cannot acquire the true knowledge of the self. Without education, the inexhaustible fund of innocent pleasure which lies in various books is also closed to us. It is no exaggeration but a statement of fact that man without learning is not far removed from an animal.

Thus, a woman, like man, needs education, not that a women should get the same kind of education as given to a man. In the first place, the education that is being given us by the Government is, to a great extent, faulty and harmful. It should therefore be eschewed by both men and women. Even if its defects were removed I would not consider it proper for women. Men and women are equal in status, but they are not the same in physical or mental make-up. They are a unique pair. They complement each other and are absolutely necessary to each other, so much so that one cannot exist without the other. It follows as a corollary from these facts that anything that will impair the status o either of them will involve the ruin of both, in equal measure.

Those who draw up plans for the education of women must remember this. Man rules the outer circle of the life of a married pair. Therefore he must have the greater knowledge of all those activities of life which constitute his sphere. The women, on the other hand is dominant in the inner or domestic circle of their life. She must have special knowledge of the management of the home, care of children, their education, etc. it is not suggested that either men or women should be forbidden from acquiring a knowledge of what belongs specially to the province of the other. But unless courses of instruction are based on a discriminating appreciation of these ideas, both men and women would be deprived of the opportunity of achieving perfection in their respective spheres.

A few words are also necessary about the question as to whether or not women need to know English. I feel that generally speaking, knowledge of

English is not necessary either for men or for women. Men might require it for earning their livelihood or for taking part in political work. But I do not believe in women working for a living or undertaking commercial enterprises. Therefore, only a few women would need to learn English. And those who want to May well learn it in the schools for men.

Introducing English in all schools for women will only lead to a prolongation of the period of our helplessness. I have often heard people say that the rich treasures of English literature should be as easily available to women as they are to men. I humbly submit that this is an erroneous view even though the error may not be evident. No one says that the treasures of English literature should be open to men but closed to women. He who loves literature may well explore the literature of the whole world. None will, or can. Stop him from doing so, if he has the necessary will. But, since we are concerned with formulating a plan to suit the needs of our people in general, we cannot attend to the special needs of a few lovers of literature.

For them there will have to be-when we are sufficiently advanced and prosperous-separate institutions for learning and research as there are in Europe. When there is a general spread of education, when most of our men and women start getting educated, we may be sure that numerous writers will rise from amongst us who will make available to us the joy of the literatures of other languages. If we continue to derive pleasure only from English literature alone, our languages will always remain poor. This means that we as a people will also remain mentally poor. I would even say, if you will forgive me for the simile, that the habit of deriving joy from the literature of another language is like that of a thief who derives joy from stolen property.

The English poet pope presented to his people, in his beautiful English, whatever joy he tasted in *Iliad;* in the same way, Fitzgerald embodied the joy he derived from the poetry of Omar Khayyam in such attractive English that millions of Englishmen love and treasure his translation of the poetry of Khayyam like their own Bible, Edwin Arnold tasted the nectar of our *Bhagavad Gita*. He did not ask his people to learn Sanskrit to experience the joy that he had experienced in that book.

On the other hand, he made it available to the people in English which is as beautiful as the original Sanskrit and in which besides he has succeeded in pouring out his very soul as it were. Seeing that we are still backward in this respect, we must pay more attention to the work of translating. But it will be possible only when we have made our plan of education along the lines I have indicated and implement it. If we give up being fascinated by

English and our distrust of the distrust of the power of our own language, this will not be difficult to achieve.

It is not necessary for any men or women to spend his or her tome learning English in order to appreciate good literature. I do not say this merely to be a wet blanket. But because I want the pleasure, which the English-educated people derive with great difficulty, made easily available to all of us through translations. The languages of the world are full of many a invaluable gem. And not all the gems of literature are in English. I want all these gems to be brought within the reach of our people. The only way to achieve this end is for those of us who have a flair for languages to learn them and then present the foreign literary classics in our own. *(Presidential speech on the occasion of the Second Annual Conference of the Bombay Bhangini Samaj, 1918 (CW 14, PP.207-09)*

Higher education for women

After primary education, a girl gets another four to five years of secondary education. Expressing his views on the question as to whether in this period she should be taught through English or the mother tongue, Gandhiji said: "I feel that teaching English to them under the circumstances would be like killing them. It will never be possible for hundreds of thousands of women to think or express their thoughts in English; and even if it were possible, it would be undesirable.

"If the women for whom we are drawing up this plan are imparted higher education through the mother tongue, they could make their homes as bright and beautiful as gold. Not only that, they could also exert their good influence on their uneducated on their uneducated sisters and thus render valuable service to them as well." (True Education, PP. 157-58)

Modern Girl's education

I was really surprised to see the stride that education among girls had taken in the state of Travancore. It was a perfect eye-opener to me. The question has always occurred to me: "what will india do with its modern girls?" I call you modern girls of India. The education that we are receiving in these institutions, in my opinion, does not correspond with the life around us, and, when I say life around us, I do not mean the life around us in the cities but the life around us in the villages. Perhaps some of you girls, if not all of you, know that real India is to be found not here in the villages. Perhaps some of you girls, if not all of you, know that real India is to be found not here in the very few cities but in the seven hundred thousand villages covering a surface of 1,900 miles long and 1,500 miles broad. The question is whether you have any message for your sisters in the villages. Men do not need the message perhaps so much as the women, and I have long before come to the conclusion that unless women of India work side by side with men, there is no salvation for India, salvation in more sense than one. I mean political salvation in the broadest sense, and I mean economic salvation and spiritual salvation also. *(Speech at Women's college, Madras, 24 March 1925 (CW 26, PP. 395-96))*

Curriculum for Girl's Education

Women must learn as part of elementary education at least their own mother tongue, Hindi if it is not their mother tongue, enough Sanskrit to be able to understand the drift of the *Bhagavad Gita*, elementary arithmetic, elementary composition, elementary music and child-care. Along with this, I think they should know well the processes up to the weaving from cotton. When a woman receives this education she should have an environment that will shape her character and enable her to see clearly the evils in society and to avoid them. I have not mentioned religious education separately as it is acquired by partice and would be covered by general reading. Truly speaking, it is a part of the elevating company of a teacher. This is about girls. The education of a widow or a married woman is of course a different matter. *(Letter to Aanandibai, 22 August 1927 (CW 34, p. 384) (Translated from Gujarati))*

Education to women

Today we have assembled for the opening of a girl's school. I have made a thorough study of child education. I could say the same thing about girl's education. But how can experts accepts this? Today, even I cannot make that claim. In the prevailing state pf affairs it is not easy to talk about girl's education. Everyone may well claim that he is capable of giving education to girls. I will however ask him whether he has imparted true education to his daughter or his wife.

How can he who has not observed his dharma towards his wife, sister, mother or mother-in-law, set out to teach the daughters or sisters of others? They may well become B.As. or M.As. But I shall put them to the same test. I should like to know what kind of husbands and fathers those who write books on girl's education are. *(Speech at Inauguration of Vithal kanya Vidyalaya, Nadiad, 31 May 1935 (CW 61, P. 118))*

Deschooling or Nai Talim?

It was said that the state of education in the world including India is facing the crises of survival. The best minds in the world are worried over the pathological state of education. We have presented a lot of empirical in India and abroad to support the validity of such a view. The educational system suffers from many and various ills, and it is harming instead of doing good to the society. Men like Gandhis have condemned the system in the strongest terms usually not found in their talks and writings.

What additional steps should we take so that educational becomes and remains the greatest, vital resources? One suggestion is that all the schools should be closed or there should be Deschooling of education? The other view is that the revolutionary transformation in the educational system through enlightened policies should be brought about. The second approach is a superior approach. The first approach would results u throwing the baby with bathwater.

Coeducation

In theory, we are quite in favor of boys and girls receiving education together. But, in practice, it is impossible to ignore deep-rooted habits or prejudices. Experiences have shown that Indian parents, as a rule, will not allow their daughters to mingle with boys at a school or elsewhere. And, whenever a forcible mixture takes place, the result is ludicrous in the extreme. Both the boys and girls feel awkward. "Let them", shouts the unthinking reformer. "They will soon be at home, if left alone." But the parents will not wait for the process. They are not reformers and they will not allow experiments to be made at their children's expenses. *(Indian Opinion, 19 August 1911 (CW 11, P. 145))*

Coeducation not compulsory

As for coeducation, the Zakir Hussain committee has not made it compulsory. Where there is a demand for a separate school for girls, the state will have to make provision. The question of coeducation has been left open. It will regulate itself according to the time-spirit. So far as I am aware the members of the committee were not all of one mind. Personally I have an open mind. I think that there are just as valid reasons for as against coeducation. And I would not oppose the experiment wherever it is made. *(Harijan, 16 July 1938 (CW 67, P. 175))*

Coeducation in training schools

Shari Avinasshilingam, the Education Minister of Madras, felt that the coeducation policy of the Talimi Sangh was not suitable to Madras. He had no objection to coeducation among children and among grown-ups, when they know their own minds. But he was not in favor of coeducation at the impressionable age of 15 or 16 when most of the girls came to training schools. Gandhiji, however, disagreed. "if you keep coeducation in your schools but not in your training schools. The children will think there is something wrong somewhere. I should allow my children to run the risk. We shall have to rid ourselves one day of this sex mentality. We should not seek for examples from the west. Even in training-schools, if the teachers are intelligent, pure and filled with the spirit of Nayee Taleem, there is no danger. Supporting if some accidents do take place, we should not be frightened by them. They would take place anywhere. Although I speak thus boldly, I am not unaware of the attendant risks. Toy, as a responsible Minister, should think of you and act accordingly." *(Harijan, 9 November 1947 (CW 89, PP. 332-33))*

GANDHI ON TEACHERS

Improve teaching methods

My ideas about education are very exacting. If we want to pour our souls into the pupils, we should constantly exercise our mind on how to teach them. We should not get angry with them. Passing on to them in the best possible language from day to day whatever we wish to give them, will take up much of our time. Moreover, we must for the present think of teaching methods as well. Everything will have to be taught in a new way.

The teachers will have to come together at least once a week to exchange ideas and make such changes as may be called for. The intelligent students should be consulted and their suggestions invited about methods of teaching.

The student's health is the collective responsibility of the teachers; the main responsibility, however, will rest on the teacher in charge of hygiene.

The teachers should read up the subjects in the curriculum which they do not know especially Hindi. I can see from my work here how very essential Hindi is. I find that I shall have to ask for volunteers from other places. Difficulties will arise about those of them who do not know Hindi. I see it proved every day that education is altogether incomplete without Hindi. *(Letter to Narahari Parikh, 17 May 1917 (CW 13, P. 399))*

Make Teaching Absorbing

Experience shows that student's interest in a subject is sustained not by the subject-matter but by the teacher. My own experience has been that one teacher used to bore me to sleep while teaching chemistry, whereas another teacher kept me wide awake and interested in the same subject. The former, who talked and talked without clarifying the topic, was not liked while, as the other teacher elucidated the theme, one wished that his period should never end. The topic was the same as well as the students. Instruction by one, however, was absorbing and by the other insipid. The spinning-wheel holds a jar or nectar. In the Darshinamurti Bhavan, there are teachers who can reveal this. *(Navajivan, 17 August 1924 (CW 25, P. 5) (Translated from Gujarati))*

Teaching for the love of it

However, the teachers have asked for advice and I can but place it before them so that each may then respond to the best of his ability. The unfortunate position is that educated Indians take to teaching not for the love of it, but because they have nothing better and nothing else for giving them a livelihood. Many of them even enter the teaching profession with a view to preparing for what they regard as a better thing. The wonder is that in spite of this self-imposed initial handicap so many teachers are not worse than they are. By well-oriented agitation, no doubt they may better their pecuniary prospective, but I see no chance even under a Swaraj government of the scale of salary being raised much higher than it is today. I believe in the ancient idea of teachers teaching for the love of it and receiving the barest maintenance.

The Roman Catholics have retained that idea amd they are responsible for some of the best educational institutions in the world. The *Rishis* of old did even better. They made their pupils members of their families, but in those days that class of teaching which they imparted was not intended for the masses. They simply brought up a race of real teachers of mankind in India. The masses got their training in their homes and in their hereditary occupations. It was a good enough ideal for those times. Circumstances have now changed. There is a general insistent demand for literary times. The masses claim the same attention as the classes. How far it is possible and beneficial to mankind generally cannot be discussed here. *(Young India, 6 August 1925 (CW 28, 34-36))*

Teacher-taught relationship

I believe in *guru-bhakti*. But every teacher cannot be a *guru*. The *guru-Shishya-* the teacher-disciple-relation in this sense is something spiritual and springs up spontaneously. In any case it is not an artificial thing or a product of pressure from without. Such teachers still exist in India. (It should not be necessary to sound the warning that I am not speaking here of spiritual teachers who have the power to lead the aspirants to liberation.) Such teachers have no use for flattery. Respect for them must be natural and so is the love of the teacher for his pupil. That being so, the teacher is ever ready to give, and the pupil equally ready to receive.

GANDHI ON MORAL EDUCATION

Teaching children virtues and values

Children are the pillar of our tomorrow is a statement that is repeated time and again. And it is an axiom; they are our pillars of the coming time. But then do we nurture them into becoming healthy human beings?

By healthy human beings here is not meant the physical wellbeing, but the good human being. And how do you define a good human being/ one with virtues and values that keeps them in the realm of working towards the benefit of humanity.

How can children imbibe within themselves the virtues and values? Well, this is the primary responsibility of parents and other immediate family members, followed by school authorities. The values and virtues of an individual is sown in their childhood and nurtured as they grow up. After all nobody is born a criminal, it is what they become as result of what they gain from their surroundings.

Depending on the way we bring up our children, we decide our own future. It is vital that in the formative years we give them quality time and attention. We teach them to discriminate between the good, bad and the ugly. We have to inculcate into them positive emotions like love and compassion and teach them actions of kindness and generosity. At the same time we have to help them do way with the negatives of hatred, anger, jealousy, selfishness, etc.

Your child is like a plant. You sow the seeds and also reap the benefits of its growth and development. First and foremost you as a parent have to realize your responsibility in nurturing a child to growing into a good human being. And it is just not anyone of the parents, but both together to inculcate the values and virtues into your child.

Teaching your child love

Love moves the world and hate stagnates it. It is all too easy to look out of the window and complain about how much hate is dominating our lives today. But then, how much love do we spread in our lives? In the present stressful existence, we have forgotten how to love each other. Frustration, stress, anger, impatience, intolerance, and reign supreme. And as a result we have children growing in an environment that is minus love and peace.

Love is the strongest emotion that brings happiness into ones lives. For us to nurture our children into becoming good human beings we must inculcate in them the emotion called love. And what is love? It may be defined as affection, devotion, fondness, admiration, compassion, attachment, dedication, etc. when we learn to live by these emotions then we do away with the negatives that cause our destruction.

We can bring into our children the emotion of love only when we create for ourselves a loving environment. As parents we firstly have to avoid bringing our bedroom fights into the drawing room. We have to have patience and tolerance and accept each other for each or our plusses and minuses. When we accept each other, then only can we teach our children the same.

Children growing up in a home where there is no love, grow into being insecure individuals. They are constantly disturbed by what happens between their parents. The constant fights and arguments instill in them fear and they do not trust the outside world. In fact these children seek attention from all over the place. They are always striving to be their best only out of insecurity. And this is a negative aspect, because at some point out of frustration they just want to stop short of everything and give up. A child not nurtured in love and affection grows into being a depressed emotional wreck who finds it difficult to adjust in society.

Remember, your Childs wellbeing, whether it is emotional, physical, psychological, mental or otherwise, depends on the environment you bring up your child in. if it is a loving one, then you are bringing up an adjusting human being. A terrorist after all is not born into a home of love and affection, but one shrouded by intense hate.

Teaching your child to respect elders

As you sow, so shall you reap? To gain respect from your children first you must respect your own elders in front of them. Not only that you have to respect each other too. We tend to take for granted that respecting each other is about enslaving each other. We consider that respect is what we give to an authority figure, because we need to be in their good books. However, that is not respect, but disrespect since it is not something genuine.

Respect towards elders or nay person, as a matter of fact is about honoring or holding in esteem an individual. It implies regarding an individual as a person of value and virtue. We all expect respect for others. But then do we actually respect others? For instance, because we are adults we tend to take our parents for granted. We tend to get irritated by every suggestion they make simply because we think that we can never be wrong.

We then admonish them or ignore them. We do not realize that our children copy or rather mimic us. They then treat us the same way.

Apart from this even the way we address the servants, is the way our children will address them too. While your servant is hired by you and you have every right to give them orders the way you want, realize that they are still elders for your children. When you ill-treat or talk with disrespect to your servant, your child does the same thing.

It is vital to teach your child how to respect each individual, in order for him or her to command his or her own respect. And it all begins with you as a parent. Another aspect we overlook is also the way we talk about people in front of our children. For instance, when we bad-mouth somebody in front of our children, they overhear our conversation, disrespect that person and put us into an embarrassing situation. So it is very vital that we watch our own actions and words in the presence of our children, otherwise it will spell trouble not only for us, but also for them, as there would be nothing beyond disrespect in the dictionary of upbringing.

GANDHI ON RELIGIOUS EDUCATION

Gandhis ideas on religious education are described in this chapter in his own words. It will provide an insight into the vastness of his vision and the expanses of his thought-process.

State versus religious instruction

If India is not to declare spiritual bankruptcy, religious instruction of its youth must be held to be at least as necessary as secular instruction. It is true that knowledge of religious books is no equivalent of that of religious. But if we cannot have religion, we must be satisfied with providing out boys and girls with what is next best. And whether there is such instruction given in the schools or not, grown-up students must cultivate the art of self-help about matters religious as about others. They may start their own class just as they have their debating, and now, spinners clubs.

I do not believe that the state can concern itself or cope with religious education. I believe that religious education must be the sole concern of religious associations. Do not mix up religion and ethics. I believe that fundamental ethics is common to all religions. Teaching of fundamental ethics is undoubtedly a function of the state. By religion I have not in mind fundamental ethics but what goes by the name of denominationalism. We have suffered enough from state-aided religion and a state Church. A society or a group, which depends partly or wholly on state aid for the existence of its religion, does not deserve, or, better still, does not have any religion worth the name.

A curriculum of religious instruction should include a study of the tenets of faiths other than one's own. For this purpose the students should be trained to cultivate the habit of understanding and appreciating the doctrines of various great religions of the world in a spirit of reverence and broad-minded tolerance.

Religious education and the teacher

You have rightly found place for religious instruction. I have experimented with quite a number of boys in order to understand how best to impart religious instruction and whilst I found that book instruction was somewhat of an aid, by itself it was useless. Religious instruction, I discovered, was imparted by teachers living the religion themselves. I have found that boys imbibe more from the teachers own lives than they do form the books that they read to them, or the lectures that they deliver to them with their lips. I have unconsciously a faculty of penetration whereby they read the thoughts of their teachers. Woe to the teacher who teaches one thing with his lips, and carries another in his breast.

Ethical teaching in schools

Should religious instruction from part of the school curriculum as approved by the state? Do you favor separate schools for children belonging to different denominations for facility of religious instruction? Or should religious instruction be left in the hands of private bodies? If so, do you think it is right for the state to subsidize such bodies?

I do not believe in state religion even though the whole community has one religion. The state interference would probably always be unwelcome. Religion is purely a personal matter. There are in reality as many religions as minds. Each mind has a different conception of God from that of the other.

I am also opposed to state aid, partly or wholly, to religious bodies. For I know that an institution or group which does not manage to finance its own religious teaching, is a strange to true religion, this does not mean that the state schools would not give ethical teaching. The fundamental ethics are common to all religious.

Religious versus fundamental virtues

To me religion means Truth and *ahimsa* or rather Truth alone, because Truth includes *ahimsa, ahimsa* being the necessary and indispensable means for its discovery. Therefore, anything that promotes the partice of these virtues is a means for imparting religious education and the best way to do this, in my opinion, is for the teachers rigorously to practice these virtues in their own person. Their very association with the boys, whether on the playground or in the classroom, will then give the pupils a fine training in these fundamental virtues.

So much for instruction in the universal essentials of religion. A curriculum of religious instruction should include a study of the tenets of faiths other than one's own. For this purpose the students should be trained to cultivate the habit of understanding and appreciating the doctrines of various great religious of the world in a spirit of reverence and broad-minded tolerance. This if properly done would help to give them a spiritual assurance and a better appreciation of their own religion. There is one rule, however, which should always be kept in mind while studying all great religion and that is that one should study them only through the writings of known votaries of the respective religious.

For instance, if one wants to study the *Bhagavata* one should do so not through a translation of it made by a hostile critic but one prepared by a lover of the *Bhagavata*. Similarly to study the Bible one should study it through the commentaries of devoted Christians. This study of other religious besides one's own will give one a grasp of the rock-bottom unity of all religions and afford a glimpse also of that universal and absolute truth which lies beyond the 'dust of creeds and faiths'. Let no one even for a moment entertain, the fear that a reverent study of other religions is likely to weaken or shake one's faith in one's own. The Hindu system of philosophy regards all religious as containing the elements of truth in them and enjoys an attitude of respect and reverence towards them all. This of course presupposes regard for one's own religion. Study and appreciation of other religions need not cause a weakening of that regard; it should mean extension of that regard to other religions.

In this respect religion stands on the same footing as culture. Just as preservation of one's own culture does not mean contempt for that of others, but requires assimilation of the best that there may be in all other cultures, even so should be the case with religion. Our present fears and apprehensions are a result of the poisonous atmosphere that has been generated in the country, the atmosphere of mutual hatred, ill-will and distrust; we are constantly laboring under a nightmare of fear lest someone should stealthily undermine our faith or the faith of those who are dear and near to us. But this unnatural state will cease when we have learnt to cultivate respect and tolerance towards other religions and their votaries.

Education for individual

For Gandhi's education should help to prepare and direct the learner towards the true purpose of life, which is to realize the Atman. The self which he views as realizing God the spiritual realization or the self realisation that Gandhi values as the major aim of life. According the Gandhiji education must prepare the learner or learners for self-realization or liberation (moksha). He emphasized the ancient Indian wisdom-Sa vidya *ya vimuktaya*. (That which liberates knowledge).In his socio-political and education thought.

Views regarding liberation – Gandhi talked about two kinds of liberations. One form of liberation consisted in securing the freedom of the country from foreign rule. Which for him would also include development indigenous models of school, economical, educational development. Such freedom however may prove short-lived if not understood in the right perspective and light of the other kind of liberation (moksha) which is for all time. As aviation he is referring to the liberation from the cycles of birth and death on the earth, from the suffering of the world, and he is emphasizing this liberation, *moksha* as the ultimate goal for life (one of the fourth purusharthas thus other three being *dharma*) *artha, Kama*. It is important to emphasize here that this liberation is an individual liberation and does not transform the earth –nature in any way.

EDUCATION FOR KNOWLEDGE

Education is considered as a process of bringing perfection in the human beings education carries out these humans and social functions by directing, guiding and reshaping the inmate potential and impulses of the child, by helping the individual in the process of growth, unfolding what is within and preparing him to assume the responsibility of adult life. But education carries out all these by introducing him to the total experiences of the human race classified into heads of knowledge. Historically speaking education has become a process of the individuals identification with a large variety of classified information grouped under particular subjects. Much emphasis was given to the communication of classified knowledge to the individual.

Gandhi defines education with reference to the holistic development of man. Gandhi gives education importance in this conception to the development of the mind. Education of the mind and the head cannot be undertaken except in its wider sense by the provision of knowledge or rather by exposing the individual to the classified heads of knowledge. Gandhi agrees that education should reflect the experience of the human race and for us, the Indians ancient culture and civilization that had developed. A knowledge of our culture and civilization becomes a main part of the education that be imparts to the new generations. Several values will thus be attached to the education individual a love for the heritage of the country. Education for knowledge further extents itself to introducing the individual to his physical and geographical environment. Education can in no way neglect introducing the learner to a system of knowledge that encompasses the learner's own environment. Education for knowledge is also known as literary. This would include the knowledge of languages and literature and a variety of other arts-oriented subjects.

EDUCATION AND LIFE EXPERIENCE

Gandhi too made life experience a center aim of education. There was all the same major difference – Dewey's Value of practical usefulness was an end itself, while for Gandhi it constituted a major means o more remote ends and consequently to the ultimate end itself . Gandhi envisaged life and its experiences from a dynamic perspective and attempted to analyze and see life in all its completeness. Gandhi's personality is one of a minute and concrete interplay perfect on every step of a long life of a craftsman like series of experiments with historical actuality in all political and existential aspects. Gandhi did not wish to leave things to chance and looked at the events of day to day life with immense care and attention. Louis Fischer says," he discovered a new dimension of action; He split the social atom and found a new source of energy.

That was a major achievement as this constituted a basis for the development of Gandhi's philosophy of life and action. Education for life-experiences in the Gandihian sense aims at presenting to the individual the varied aspects of what we practical life in which the individual is expected to make a life of his own. The individual provided with opportunities to know for himself the intrinsic of action. Unless this aspect is brought into focus, ordinarily education does not lay stress on this right from the beginning of education the individual should be helped to undertake introspection, reasoning and analysis of his own action and those he sees around. Basically this is an ability that renders him quite different from the animals living around him. By stressing this aspect an education is helping the individual to undertake something proper to man as man. He becomes able to exercise his rational mind on everything around him, accept or reject things and experiences that life ordinarily presents to him. This would mean the individual learn to value in every step during his whole life. A link is established between the times and becomes available to one self and the series of responsibility and duties one is expected to carry out. For Gandhi life experience constitute the primary means to gain the full flowering the individual personality for the betterment of oneself, society and God.

IMPORTANCE OF DISCIPLINE

"If the boys and girls do not learn discipline in their school days, money and time spend on their education is a national loss" He talks about education in terms of discipline. It is regarded as one of the most important parts and parcels of education. Without discipline, the sound education system is impossible. It is a quality that one's self can lead to the regulation of one's intellectual, moral, spiritual and social behavior. It is stated that the goal of education consists of character-building. Such character-building requires the moral, intellectual and social behavior under all circumstances i.e., strength of personality, the virtue of compassion, kindness, fair-mindedness and the spirit of dedication. Gandhi strongly holds that education is not end in itself but it is the most powerful weapon which creates all people of genuine characters. There is degeneration of education when the qualities of truthfulness, firmness, tolerance are absence from it. True education is life process which helps in cultivating the spirit of co-operation, tolerance, public spirit and a sense of human personality. Such discipline can create the harmonious balance between the individuals and social aim of education. His principle of 'learning by doing' tries to stimulate the individual's mind to think creatively, independently and critically. His great emphasis on work-culture to the students from the primary stage to higher stage is to enable the students to start producing from the time he started his training. So, his primary information of basic education is Head, Heart and Hand rather than Reading, Writing and Arithmetic system try to develop the individual soul and mind, courage and self-reliance, cultivate the highest intellectual, moral and ethical accomplishments.

GANDHI AND POST-INDEPENDENT EDUCATION IN INDIA

Interest in basic education waned, after Gandhis death, for several reasons. The number of basic schools came down. But the massage of Gandhi was clear and it tolled steadily against the over-academic nature of formal education. He had vehemently repeated the Clarion Call for according a status to work in the curriculum. His message was honoured by the Kothari commission in its recommendation for work-experience in school education as an integral part of the curriculum. Advocating work-experience, the report observed that: "in our country, a revolutionary experiment was launched by Mahatma Gandhi in the form of basic education. The concept of work experience is essentially similar. It may be described as a redefinition of his educational thinking in terms of a society launched on the road to industrialization". Even now it is accommodated in the form of socially useful productive work.

SCOPE OF GANDHIAN EDUCATION

Gandhi and his teachings are today assuming new dimensions of meaning and relevance as we have seen in the forgoing section. The dynamic nature of Gandihian thoughts and practices is leading the whole thing to a new level of acceptance by the world community. Gandhism is thus evolving into an integrated and comprehensive discipline because of the great scope it offers for application to a variety of fields of knowledge, have the new term :' Gandihian Studies.' The intention is not to evolve yet another field of knowledge for brain storming work in theory, but Gandihian Studies is primarily an integrated, multi-pronged approach to present Gandhi to the world on the one hand and on the other, know Gandhi ever deeper with reference to the problems india in particular and the world at large are facing. A Gandihian study is an attempt in theory work and research into the holistic appeal Gandhi has made to the world in the renewal of the human spirit. It amounts, again, to a search for the of science that have become characteristic to the present age of science and technology in an attempt to discover the system of values that are detrimentally forgotten.

Gandihian Studies offers considerable scope for us "to prove that Gandhi's entire scheme of action was to strengthens, organize and develop the potentials for good present in individuals and in society and thus defeat evil at all levels". This fundamental aim of all activities of Gandhi to fight the forces of evil at all levels and nurture good sown in the sands and hearts of Indians is seldom understood in the right perspective. The aim of the present discipline therefore is to provide full scope in understanding Gandhi in this perspective. Modern India must be concertized in regard to the Gandihian interpretation of the meaning of life and must develop an awareness of the full practical political o Gandihian thoughts and viewpoints. Gandihian has a message for everyone, belonging to all walks of life and this message should receive to the present day needs.

Gandhi wanted Indians to be fully conscious of the rural nature of our country. India meant rural India and all his thoughts rested with the working and agricultural population of rural India. The greatest justice that we may do to him is to accept rural India as it is study the problems of this vast population, recognize the potentials available at their disposal and thereby present rural India to the vision of the more affluent factions of the country . It was Gandhi's earnest desire to introduce students to the manifold problems of rural India and develop in them a sustaining love for them vacation. Gandhi said, "Student should spend every day of their vocation in the villages around their school and colleges" there is no relation between today's education and our family life. Gandihian studies incorporate knowledge of and work in villages to develop in students a love for these villages. These will enable students to:

A. Acquaint themselves to rural India,

B. Constructively study rural problems,

C. Correlate such problems with their own personal life and views

D. Set out to investigate into aspects and areas for helping life in villages.

E Develop schemes and plans of a comprehensive nature for rural upliftment. Gandihian studies can focus on such issues in a productive manner.

Gandhian studies offers scope for interdisciplinary learning and research. This discipline becomes highly interdisciplinary because of its very texture. It subscribes as many disciplines for work and development as covered by Gandhism itself. Gandhian thoughts cover a variety of fields due to its comprehensiveness and thereby relate itself to those areas of knowledge and practice as the stem of a tree to its branches. No study of Gandhi, for instance is possible without relating itself to the field of education because Gandhian gets itself rooted in educational goals, principles, values and practices. A presentation of a training in the educational principles and practices Gandhi held as dear can be possible only by developing these within a more comprehensive study of education to avoid random and piece meal work. This approach makes it necessary to include as inter disciplines subjects within whose wider framework alone can Gandhian studies be developed.

Under this approach Gandhian studies includes political science. No understanding of Mahatma Gandhi can be possible without an analysis of Gandhi's political career that led to India's Independence. The Politician in Gandhi has received worldwide acclaim because of the unique way he conducted himself and developed his Political Philosophy. It is significant to see that Gandhi had no Political Philosophy separated from his central religious Phenomenology. He said, "I was compelled to come into Political because I was convinced that without touching Political one will not be able to do any form of social service." Especially in the circumstances in which Gandhi worked, he was convinced that no spiritual or religious pursuit could be possible without entering into political. Here we find already how the two field's study of Gandhism would therefore amount to acquainting or e self with the fundamental of political science that formed the basis of Gandhi's political involvements. That would also lead to the various influences on Gandhi's political thought and the details of the political theory of Mahatma Gandhi. The student should have also an opportunity to critically examine the merits and relevance of the Gandhian political system.

FEATURE OF BASIC EDUCATION

Basic education is the foundational education, fundamental to the whole scheme of education meant for "an all-round development of the child and man-body, mind and spirit. It is 'basic' in nature because it attempts to given the minimum of learning to be acquired by an average child. It is correlated with the basic needs of the child, the food, clothing, shelter, clean and healthy living etc. It is also intimately related to the basic occupations of the community. It also comes just in time that is at the primary stage of education. However, later on, the shape of Basic Education was widened to include pre-Basic, Post-Basic, and Adult education, besides the Basic stage.

According to Prof. K.L Shrimali and others, the fundamental features of the scheme as outlined by Mahatma Gandhi are-

1. Free and compulsory Education. It implies a free and compulsory.
2. Purposeful activity. Basic Education centers on some purposeful activity or a useful and productive craft.
3. Medium of Instruction. The medium of Education in the mother tongue of the child.
4. Dignity of labour. It inculcates the virtues of dignity of labour, a keen sense of discipline and a great sense of responsibility.
5. Self-supporting. It is self-supporting. Children learn by doing. In it, the craft has both an educational and economic value. Children learn from their craft work and through it, they cover their expenses.
6. Village-oriented. It was primarily devised for village. According Gandhiji, "In the villages, the bulk of India's population resides. So, to tackle successfully, the question of villages is to solve the problem for the cities also.
7. New co-operative regime. Basic education aims at bringing about a new co-operative regime in place of the present in human regime based on exploitation and violent forces.
8. Integrated teaching. In Basic education, all the subjects are taught in an integrated way. All the instruction is correlated with craft or the natural and social environments.

9. Co-operative work. In Basic education, both the teachers and the pupils work for community development and social progress.
10. All round development of the child. Basic Education is meant to educate the body, mind and spirit of the child. In all, it seeks to develop the child as a whole.

LIMITATIONS, SHORTCOMINGS OF BASIC EDUCATION OR NAI TALIM

Like other contributions of Gandhi, this idea of basic education (BE) also has been severely criticized by certain scholars. On further thinking, it would be found that a lot of misunderstanding, dogmatism underlies the criticism.

1. It has been said that BE idea is based on unsound psychological foundation. Human Nature has three aspects-cognitive, affective, and conative. BE emphasizes that last aspect but ignores the first.
2. It is impossible to establish any natural association between craft and all the subjects of cultural values. It is assured to hang all knowledge to the peg of a single craft.
3. Education suited to our national genius would have definite religious basis. Craft-centered education is decidedly alien to our ancient ideals.
4. BE is not suited to industrialized social order or an age of industrialization. This criticism springs from the static and not dynamic set up. A new educational system will be working in changing levels of industrialism.
5. The scheme will introduce too much of a ruinous competition.
6. The insensitive approach by intellectuals has led them to heap certain epithets and condemn the philosophy of Nai Talim. For example, BE is fraud which is being committed on the nation by those who are in power.
7. It is a sort of political stunt to play with the sentiments of the people.
8. BE is a fallacy. The very fundamentals are wrong.
9. BE is a farce. It is impracticable.
10. BE is a fad. It has no sound psychological and pedagogical basis.

Why has Nai Talim not given results? This scheme of education has not produced any tangible far-reaching results. Although the new scheme has many merits, (it contacts Gandhi's penetrating vision; it cuts all the fruitless verbiage discussions) it could be revolutionize the Indian Educational system. In fact, the initial response of the people was highly discouraging, dishearting. The scheme of Nai Talim was first published in Harijan in 1937 in the form of articles. When these articles were first published, there was a storm of protests in educational circles. People who had worked in the seclusion of their offices and files were thrown off their balance. These ideas were opposed and dubbed as entirely impractical. The system in India then and now also has been more and more book-centered; it did not help to develop intellect, emotions, and character.

The sub-committee of the 1937 conference was in favour of a broad liberal curriculum for elementary education and expression of facilities for technical education. Financial responsibility for compulsory primary education was assigned to be that of the state.

In contrast to Gandhi's utopia of village republics enjoying considerable autonomy, the modernist utopia featured a strong centralized state responsible for building an industrial infrastructure in order to ensure a high standard of living for all. Nehru agreed with the main pedagogical assumptions underlying basic education, namely, a craft or manual activity stimulates the child's mind.

Now, it may be remembered that all responses to Nai Talim were not hostile. Many eminent educationists that the idea of BE, and many extensive plans to implement such ideas were prepared. Despite the range in the interpretations that the Nai Talim proposal, the scheme of basic schools was implemented on the considerable scale in several parts of India after independence. However, the implementation of BE scheme could not survive the "development decade" of 1960's when the Indian company and its politics entered into the phase featuring centralization of power, and so on.

SUMMING UP GANDHIJI VIEW ON EDUCATION

It is not quite fair to limit Gandhis philosophy and principles of education to basic system of education. His contribution goes far beyond. Basic system of education is just one of the contributions of education. There is no dimension of life and education on which Gandhi has not expressed his views. His views on the importance of mother tongue as medium of instruction, his emphasis on manual labour, and his stress on 'learning by earning', his views on the significance of women's education and the role of the teacher etc. are quite relevant today.

To Gandhiji, education was an integral part of a comprehensive programme of socio-economic re-constructed of Indian society.

As a political and spiritual leader and an economic and social reformer, Gandhiji was naturally concerned with education. All his constructive programmers, economic, educational, ethical, political, social and spiritual were organically interconnected. Gandhiji wrote: "My life is indivisible whole and all my activities run into one another, and they all have their rise in my insatiable love for mankind".

Chapter 4
Gandian Approach to experiential learning

HISTORICAL PERSPECTIVE

The freedom movement emphasized on two aspects while exploring elementary education, one was to universalize the elementary education and the second was that education needs to be qualitatively different from that which was given during the colonial times. In 1906, the Indian National Congress called for 'a system of education which is scientific and technical, suited to the requirements of the country'. It was addressing the essential concern of the colonial tendency which was reinforcing social fragmentation. They sought for a system of education which would not promote dichotomy between the work and education. They challenged the colonial masters.

In the National Education Conference held at Wardha in October, 1937, Gandhi gave a shape to a national system of education which emerged as alternative educational paradigm. The Conference deliberated upon Gandhis proposal of Basic Education (Buniyadi Shiksha) which would make productive work a pedagogic basis of learning in schools. Learning in a cooperative mode by viewing schools as communities engaged in production and making schools self-reliant through the income of productive work were amongst the other key features of the original proposal that was viewed as a means of social transformation. The pedagogic vision of Nai Talim was that of education being holistic.

Those who work with their hands and produce wealth are denied access to formal education, their work gets degraded to being manual and being bereft of skills. Today schools continue to accentuate the divide between work and knowledge. While carrying the legacy of colonial education, a disjuncture gets created between the 'valid' textbook knowledge provided at school and the learning inherent in productive work. Most schooling experience however not only ignores this source of experiential learning but also denigrates it as being inferior and thus alienates a child from it. Today we find instances of the parents lamenting that the children are refusing to work in the field after school. Many parents do not even expect their school educated children to work in the field these days in most of our villages. This accentuates a set of social ethos.

What made the exclusion of skills and values that are inherent and innate to humans? The forces of globalization continue to create privileges to the white-collared, urban, middle classes and elite. Over a period of time and systematically education in schools got disconnected from work. The education system tends to 'certify' textual knowledge as being the only 'valid' form. Thus, the knowledge inherent among the vast productive forces in the country along with its related values and skills got excluded from the school curriculum. The traditions of Pestalozzi, Owen, Tolstoy and Dewey and Gandhi's proposal for Basic Education (Buniyaadi Shiksha) challenged hierarchical-colonial paradigm. They made productive manual work as the foundation of the entire schooling experience, in asking for an integration of the head, heart and hand in the teaching-learning processes at school

According to Gandhiji: "What I am going to place before you today is not about a vocation that is going to be imparted alongside education. Now, I wish to say that whatever is taught to children, all of it needs to be taught necessarily through the medium of a trade or a handicraft. You may argue that, during the Middle Ages, children were taught only trades (crafts) in our country. While I agree with this contention, but the proposition of imparting the whole of education through the medium of trades (crafts) was not considered in those days. A trade (craft) was taught only from the standpoint of a trade (craft). We aim at developing the intellect also with the aid of a trade or a handicraft. . . . . . . Therefore, it is my submission that, instead of merely teaching a trade or a handicraft, we may as well educate the children entirely through them. Look at takli (spindle) itself, for instance. The lesson of this takli will be the first lesson of our students through which they would be able to learn a substantial part of the history of cotton, Lancashire and the British Empire. . . . . . . How does this Takli work? What is its utility? And what are the strengths that lie within it? Thus the child learns all this in the midst of play. Through this he also acquires some knowledge of mathematics. When he is asked to count the number of cotton threads on takli and he is asked to report how many did he spin, it becomes possible to acquaint him step by step with good deal of mathematical knowledge through this process. And the beauty is that none of this becomes even a slight burden on his mind. The learner does not even become aware that he is learning. While playing around and singing, he keeps on turning his takli and from this itself he learns a great deal." – *Excerpted from the address by Mahatma Gandhi at the Wardha Education Conference, 22 October 1937[Translated from Hindi, Hindustani Talimi Sangh, 1957, pp. vii-viii]*

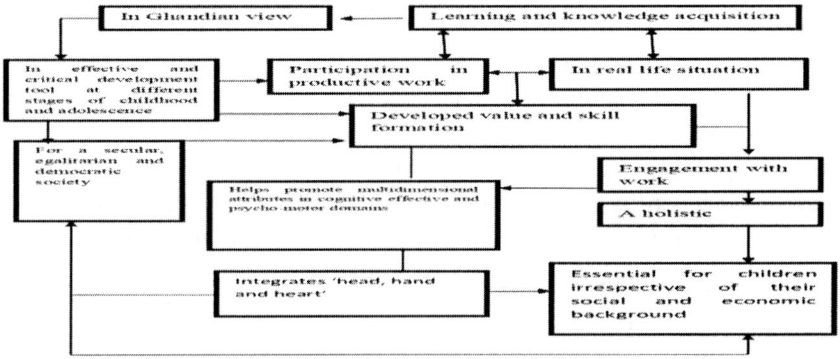

The idea of work and education has been experimented with through various initiatives all over the world. And while the benefits of the pedagogic role of work in education cannot be denied, these experiments have never been adopted as the way in which mainstream education can be taken ahead. The same is true for India. Both policy and curricular documents in India acknowledge the indelible role of work in education but do not see it as the centre of all curricular activity.

WORK EXPERIENCE

The commission clearly states that 'work- experience is...a method of integrating education and work'. It further states that Work-experience "can help to make the distinction between intellectual and manual work less marked as also the social stratification based on it. It could make the entry of youth into the world of work and employment easier by enabling them to adjust themselves to it. It could contribute to the increase of national productivity both by helping students to develop insights into productive processes and the use of science, and by generating in them the habit of hard and responsible work. And it might help social and national integration by strengthening the links between the individual and the community and by creating bonds of understanding between the educated persons and the masses." – *Report of the Education Commission (1964-66), Sections 1.27-1.29*

The benefits of integrating work and education that the report lays down- affect social inequalities by introducing children to the world of work. They hint at the potential of cognitive, social and affective learning of the child while at work. It however does not link curricular areas like Language, Mathematics and Science to work.

The report also clearly distinguishes between work experience and vocational subjects of education stating that 'a strong vocational basis needs to be given to secondary education'. However, the National Policy on Education–1986 is much more concerned with students' 'entry into the workforce' and pre-vocational programmers to "facilitate the choice of the vocational course at the higher secondary stage" than talking about the pedagogic role of work in education. The underlying premise seems to be that work-experience is meant for building the workforce and vocational courses. This confusion is at the root of the widespread tendency to equate vocational education with work-based education and vice-versa.

This concern is being articulated here precisely because the prevailing curricula in various school systems neither reflect Basic Education's vision of a work-centered curriculum nor the Education Commission's conception of work-experience. And, in popular perception as also in academic discourse, work-experience is often confused with vocational education, something which Gandhiji, as quoted above, warned us about in his address to the Wardha Conference in 1937!

COMMUNITY WORK AND SOCIAL ACTION

The Kothari Commission (1964-66) considered social service as one of the basic elements for a good and purposeful education and recommended that "some form of social and national service needs to be made obligatory for all students and needs to form an integral part of education at all stages (Sections 1.39-1.40)." The Ishwarbhai Patel Committee Report (1977), while reviewing NCERT's ten-year school curriculum framework (1975), observed that the curriculum needs to be capable of relating learning "closely to socially productive manual work and the socioeconomic situation of the country" and making it available "in such a way that working and learning can always be combined." Preferring the term "purposive, meaningful, manual work" in the curriculum as Socially Useful Productive Work (SUPW), the Committee observed: "The purpose of demarcating a distinct curricular area as Socially Useful Productive Work is to emphasize the principle that education needs to be work-centred . . . . The aim of this curricular area is to provide children with opportunities of participating in social and economic activities inside and outside the classroom, enabling them to understand scientific principles and processes involved in different types of work and in the setting in which they are found in the physical and social environment

. . . . .[it] needs to not be confined to the four walls of the school, nor can they be provided by the teacher only. Programmes needs to, therefore, be so planned and implemented that the local community, community development organisations and governmental agencies participate in them and cooperate with the school." *Report of the Review Committee on "The Curriculum for the Ten-Year School" (1977), Chapter 3, pp. 10-11.*

Thus, while SUPW talked about productive, manual work being used for community work and social service it also did not envision of a work-centered curriculum. Furthermore, as our school system is too structured (timetable, textbooks, examinations) to allow for space for the initiatives thought of, SUPW classes in schools get reduced to being hobby classes. In fact, the terms Work Experience and SUPW have come to be used interchangeably in schools.

SCHOOL CURRICULUM, EXPERIENTIAL LEARNING AND WORK EDUCATION

Work is a part of the childhood of most Indian children. Children participate in tasks like cooking, cleaning, sweeping, gardening as well sometimes in farming, pottery, carpentry, stitching and weaving of various products, fishing, food processing etc.. Children learn not only the aforesaid skills in this process but also various social and affective competencies like cooperative working in a group, tolerance, respect, discipline, creativity, effective communication, aesthetics and entrepreneurship-cum-social accountability, in this process. For many children such experiences are not natural and there is no space for the variety of these works in the teaching-learning process at school. This leads the school to devalue work with hands and instills in children a feeling of disregard for it.

The idea of work therefore, has little respect and almost no place in the curriculum. The school program and culture is textbook-centered. The idea of learning through productive, manual work is alien to our education system and the knowledge that is 'certified' is that which is prescribed in textbooks representing the dominant castes and classes. The notion of 'ideal childhood'(characterized by innocence, vulnerability and absolute dependency on adults) and 'normal child' (upper caste, upper class non-disabled male, most likely from the Hindi heartland) as supported by the textbook writers, and illustrators, policy planners, teacher-educators as well as the visual culture (TV, Photography) in most societies; the middle class academia and bureaucracy as well as the international child welfare organizations see Vasanta, 2004 for a detailed discussion) also falls within this paradigm. As a result, only lip-service has been given to making work a part of the school curriculum over the years. Spaces for work-experience and Socially Useful Productive Work (SUPW) that have been created by policy documents have trivialized the concept and reduced it to merely art and craft activities or hobbies.

Why does "need to work" be made a part of the curriculum? The school timetable for classes 3 to 10 needs to make space for exposing children to various types of work and for realizing its pedagogic potential. This position paper describes the pedagogic potential of work in terms of the following competencies.

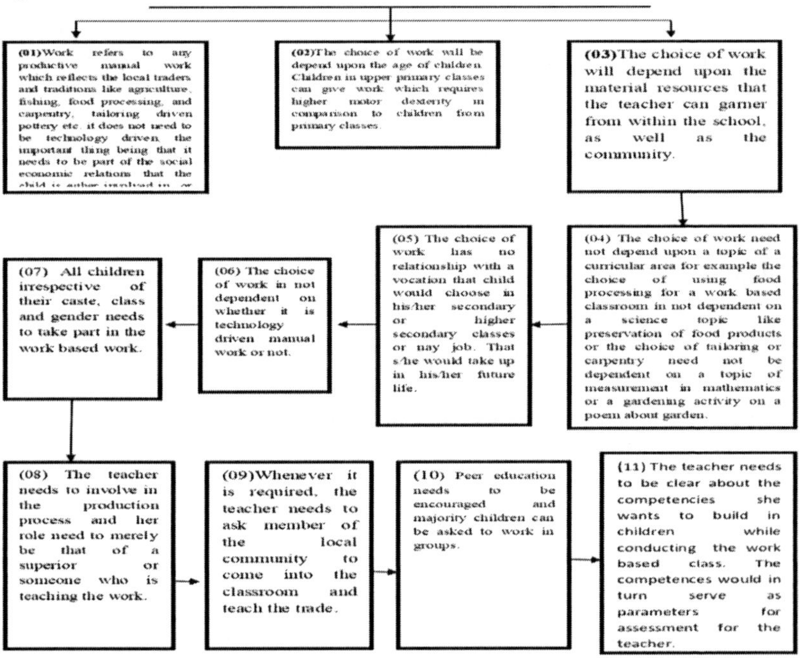

CRAFTS-CENTRIC EDUCATION FOR SKILLING

Our efforts at rectifying the imbalance in our education system through empowering potential of skilling finds a deep connect with Gandihian principles of craft-centered education. Whatever we are striving for – learning by doing, work integrated learning, respect for manual skills, self-reliance through sustainable livelihoods, – concepts like these are deeply ingrained in Mahatma Gandhi' s emphasis on manual and productive work as integral to basic education. Let's look at some of his key thoughts and ideas that have found a way in current endeavors to link education with employment and entrepreneurship through skill development.

EDUCATION THROUGH CRAFTS

Mahatma Gandhi had emphasized that handicrafts should be taught "not merely for production work but for developing intellect of the pupils." And, this idea has been implemented in schools as Socially Useful and Productive Work (SUPW) as per reports of landmark commissions and policy. SUPW is mostly perceived as a hobby; it could be embroidery, clay modeling, bamboo crafts, leather work, pottery and many other socio-culturally relevant creatively stimulating activities that have a potential for enabling livelihoods. When connected with skilling and vocational options, SUPW can transform the way children perceive manual work and impact their young minds positively towards dignity of work and labour.

The uniqueness of this scheme is that education is to be given through village crafts. The need for a machine-less society, Gandhi developed his ideas on education. The core of his proposal was the introduction of productive handicrafts in the school curriculum. The idea was not simply to introduce handicrafts as a compulsory school subject, but to make the learning of a craft the centre piece of the entire teaching programme. Knowledge of the production processes involved in crafts, such as spinning, weaving, leather-work, pottery, metal-work, basket-making and bookbinding had been the monopoly of specific caste groups in the lowest stratum of the traditional social hierarchy.

Craft is to be the center of education. Gandhiji believed that the highest development of mind and the soul was possible only through handicraft. The education of the child should begin with a useful and productive craft. Craft should form the nucleus of all instruction.

But handicraft should not be taught mechanically but scientifically. The craft should aim at developing the intellect of the pupils. With the introduction of a useful craft as the center of all instruction every school can be made self-supporting.

By teaching craft, Gandhis object was not to produce craftsmen but he wanted to exploit the craft for educative purposes. The teaching of all subjects, Gandhiji said, should be inspired by craft. The whole process of education should be imparted through it. The brain must be educated through the hand.

Benefits of craft-centered education

Craft-centered education creates a balance between theory and monotonous learning through creative stimulation and self-expression. It helps in reducing discrimination between manual and intellectual skills and overcoming prejudices through respect for socially meaningful work that meets the needs of urban and rural Indians. It makes one feel proud about earning a decent livelihood through sustainable sources of income and community initiatives that result in cooperative societies and micro enterprises

Development of Craft

According to Gandhiji, in order to train the whole men, education needs to be craft centered, because it develops skills among the students and further it leads them to be self-sufficient. Craft centered education lays emphasis on experience and activities as well as correlation of subjects with verities of crafts. It helps to develop an all round personality, in which knowledge, action and feelings are evenly balanced. The children after completing their course of education should be able to earn their livelihood. He also suggested integration of crafts in curriculum not only to use craft s an isolated practice but as a means of livelihood.

The curriculum aims at the all-round development of the learner should have the following:

- A basic craft in accordance with the local needs and conditions.
- Mother tongue is the medium of instruction.
- Arithmetic
- Social studies: General science including nature study, botany, zoology, physiology, hygiene, chemistry and physical culture.
- Art work
- Music
- Domestic science for girls.

Mahatma Gandhi had emphasized that handicrafts should be taught "not merely for production work but for developing intellect to the pupils" And, this idea has been implemented in schools as socially useful and productive work (SUPW) as per reports of landmark commissions and policy. SUPW is mostly perceived as a hobby; it could be embroidery, clay modeling, bamboo craft, leather work, pottery and many other socio culturally relevant creativity stimulating activities that have a potential for enabling livelihoods. When connected with skilling and vocational options. SUPW can transform the way children perceive manual work and impact their young minds positively towards dignity of work and labour.

WARDHA SCHEME

Origin of Wardha scheme of education

The origin of basic system of education may be traced back to July 1937 when Gandhiji wrote in Harijan (a journal started by him); "by education, I mean an all-round development drawing out of the best in child and man-body, mind and spirit. Literary itself is no education. I would, therefore, begin the child's education by teaching it a useful handicraft and enabling it to produce form the moment it begins its training. Thus every school can be made self-supporting, the condition being that the state takes over the manufacture of these schools".

In October, 1937 a Conference of National Workers was held at Wardha under the chairmanship of Mahatma Ghandi. His ideas were considered and the following resolutions passed;-

1. That in the opinion of this conference free and compulsory education be provided for seven years on a nation-wide scale.
2. That the medium of instruction be the mother-tongue.
3. That the conference endorses the proposal made by Mahatma Gandhi, that the process of education throughout this period should centre round some productive form of manual labour, and that all other abilities to be developed, or training to be given should, as far as possible, be integrally related to the environment of the child.
4. That the conference expects that the system of education will gradually be able to cover the remuneration of the child.

Zakir Hussain Committee on Basic Education: Formation of the Scheme: the conference appointed a committee under the chairmanship of Dr. Zakir Hussain, a renowned educationist. The report of the committee was published in 1938. The report is known as Wardha Scheme of Education. The scheme was approved by Mahatma Gandhi and accepted by the Indian National Congress.

Historical Background

The Government of India Act, 1935 came into force in 1937. According to the Act, Congress Ministries were formed in seven provinces in India. Prior to this Congress had been strongly pleading for free, compulsory and universal education. After having the power the Congress had to implement it in action.. Gandhiji was fully conversant with the deplorable condition of education in the land. For improving this condition he advocated a scheme of primary education based on Indian traditional culture through the medium of mother tongue. But this required a huge sum of money which meant fresh taxation.. To end this dilemma Gandhiji put forward the proposal that the plan of mass education need not be held up for want of funds. Free and compulsory primary education could be given to every child if the process of schooling could be made self-supporting by imparting education through a useful and productive craft. Gandhiji expressed his views on education through a series of articles in 'Harijan' in June 31, 1937, which later on developed into the Wardha Scheme of Basic Education. The views of Gandhiji created controversies in the academic circles. Therefore it was desirable to get the scheme examined by experts and educationists. Finally, Gandhiji placed his Basic Education System to the nation in the Wardha Conference in 1937.

Wardha Education Conference

For the purpose of discussing different aspects of the proposed new scheme of education, an All India Education Conference was held in Wardha on 22nd and 23rd October, 1937. The eminent educationists, congress leaders and workers along with the Education Ministers of the seven states had attended the conference. Gandhiji himself presided over it. After serious discussions the following four resolutions were passed.

1) That in the opinion of this Conference, free and compulsory education be provided for seven years on a nation-wide scale;
2) That the medium of instruction be the mother-tongue;
3) That the conference endorses the proposal, made by Mahatma Gandhi, that the process of education throughout this period should centre around some productive form of manual work, and that all other abilities to be developed or training should be given, as far as possible, be integrally related to the central handicraft chosen with due regard to the environment of the child.
4) That the conference expects that the system of education will be gradually able to cover the remuneration of the teachers.

Appointment of a Committee The conference appointed a committee of distinguished educationists under the chairmanship of Dr. Zakir Hussain, the Committee consisted of nine members.

- Prof. K. G. Saiidain
- Arya Nayakam,
- Vinova Bhave,
- Kaka Kalelkar,
- J. C. Kumarappa,
- Kishori Lal,
- Prof. K. T. Shah etc.

The report of the committee published in March 1938, has come to be known as the Wardha Scheme of Education. It was approved by Mahatma Gandhi and was placed before the Indian National Congress at its Haripura Session held in March 1938. The Congress accepted the scheme.

The first report included the basic principles of the Wardha Scheme of education, its aims, teachers and their training, organization of schools, administration, inspection and inclusion of craft centred education regarding handicrafts like spinning, weaving etc. The second report dealt with Agriculture, Metal work, Wood craft and other basic handicraft. An elaborate curriculum of all those subjects and ways and means to establish their correlation with other subjects was also suggested.

In course of time more conferences were held, more committees were formed on this important subject. As a result more new features were added to this aspect of education which later on took the final shape. The conference of 1945 at Sebagram characterized Basic Education as "education for life". The conference considered it as a radical and important revolution in social and economic structure of the Indian society, i.e., creating a new way of life." Since then Basic education came to be known as 'Nai Talim'. A conference of education ministers and educational workers was called by B.G. Kher in 1946 that took some important resolutions which affected the quality of Basic Education in different provinces. Basic Education has finally emerged after a decade of experimentation and discussion.

Main Features of the Wardha Scheme

The fundamental features of the scheme which was evolved in due course are as follows:

Free and compulsory education:

Gandhiji wanted education to be free and compulsory for all boys and girls between the ages of seven to fourteen. He evolved a scheme of education which would be in harmony with the culture and civilization of the Indian people and which would solve the problem of mass education in a practical way.) Free and compulsory education to be given for 8 years (from 6 to 14 years) in two stages, instead of 7 to 14. The junior stage covering 5 years and the senior 3 years.

Craft Centred Education:

The basic idea of this scheme is to impart education through some craft or productive work. Craft work helps the child to acquire sensor and motor co-ordination and to appreciate the value of honest labour. Gandhiji was of the opinion that the method of training the mind through village handicraft from the beginning as the central focus would promote the real, disciplined development of the mind. The advantages of making craft as the centre of education as listed by the Zakir Hussain Committee are as follows—

- "Psychologically, it is desirable, because it relieves the child from the tyranny of a purely academic and theoretical instruction against which its active nature is always making a healthy protest."
- "Secondly, the introduction of such practical productive work in education, to be participated in by all children of the nation will tend to break down the existing barriers of prejudice between manual and intellectual workers harmful alike for both."
- "Economically, carried out intelligently and efficiently, the scheme will increase the productive capacity of our workers and will also enable them to utilize their leisure advantageously."
- "From educational point of view, greater concreteness and reality can be given to the knowledge acquired by children through craft as knowledge will be related to life."

Self-supporting aspect of the Scheme:

The self-supporting aspect of the scheme may be interpreted in two ways—

(a) Education that will help one to be self-supporting in later life,

(b) Education which in itself is self-supporting.

The basic idea of Gandhiji was that if the craft chosen is taught efficiently or thoroughly, it would enable the school to pay the cost of salaries of teachers. At the same time his aim was to accord dignity of labour and ensure modest and honest and livelihood for the student after leaving school.

Medium of instruction:

One of the resolutions that were adopted at the All India National Conference at Wardha was that education must be imparted through the mother tongue. In this connection, the Zakir Hussain Committee's observation was that the proper teaching of the mother tongue is the foundation of all education. Without the capacity to speak effectively and to read and to write correctly and lucidly, no one can develop precision of thought or clarity of ideas. Moreover, it is a means of introducing the child to the rich heritage of his people's ideas, emotions and aspirations.

Ideal of citizenship:

Another important feature of the basic scheme is the ideal of citizenship which is implicit in it. It aimed at giving the citizens of the future a keen sense of personal growth, dignity and efficiency and social services in a cooperative community. The Zakir Hussain Committee envisaged that the new generation must at least have an opportunity of understanding their own problems and rights and obligations. A completely new system is necessary to secure the minimum of education for the intelligent exercise of the rights and duties of citizens.

Flexible Curriculum and free Environment:

The flexibility of the curriculum and free environment for the child to perform according to his own capacity are another remarkable features of basic education. Under this scheme the teachers and students are free to work according to their interest and there is no compulsion for completing a prescribed portion due to fear of examinations. Necessary changes may be introduced in the curriculum if a situation demands. Thus, whatever the child learns according to his interest and capacity is permanently remembered by him. The teacher is also free to organize necessary environment for the development of the child.

EVALUATION OF THE WARDHA SCHEME OF EDUCATION

Merits of Wardha Scheme

I. Craft Work in School:

Modern educational thought is practically unanimous in commending the idea of educating children through some suitable form of productive work. This method is considered to be the most effective approach to the problem of providing an integral all-sided education. It is useful on account of the following:

1) Psychologically, it is desirable, because it relieves the child from the tyranny of a purely academic and theoretical instruction against which its active nature is always making a healthy protest.

It balances the intellectual and practical elements of experience, and may be made an instrument of educating the body and the mind in coordination.

2) Socially considered, It is also productive as it is based on the principle of work. Work occupies the central place in basic education. The system is production oriented and helps in the programme of national reconstruction the introduction of such practical productive work in education, to be participated in by all the children of the nation, will tend to break down the existing barriers of prejudice between manual and intellectual workers, harmful alike for both. It will also cultivate in the only possible way a true sense of dignity of labor and of human solidarity – an ethical and moral gain of incalculable significance.

3) The scheme is financially sound and acceptable in a poor country like India, where about half of the total illiterate people of the world reside. It is helpful for rapid expansion of elementary education with less burden on public exchequer Economically considered, carried out intelligently and efficiently, the scheme will increase the productive capacity of our workers and will also enable them to utilize their leisure advantageously.

4) From the strictly educational point of view greater concreteness and reality can be given to the knowledge acquired by children by making some significant craft the basis of education. Knowledge will thus become related to life, and its various aspects will be correlated with one another.

II. Activity Curriculum:

In order to work out an effective and natural coordination of the various subjects and to make the syllabus a means of adjusting the child intelligently and actively to his environment, the Wardha Scheme laid stress on three centers, intrinsically inter-connected, as the foci for the curriculum, i.e. the Physical Environment, the Social Environment, and Craft Work, which is their natural meeting point since it utilizes the resources of the former for the purpose of the latter.

The Wardha Scheme of Education attempted to draft an 'activity curriculum', which implies that our school must be places of work, experimentation and discovery, not of passive absorption of information imparted at second hand. It stressed this principle by advocating that all teaching should be carried on through concrete life situations relating to craft or to social and physical environment, so that whatever a child learns becomes assimilated into his growing activities.

III. Learning by Doing:

Learning by doing sums up the educational methods of basic education. It is absolutely wrong to think that true education is acquired from books alone. There are other methods and sources which are more helpful in acquiring true knowledge. 'Chalk' and 'Talk' lessons are also not very useful. All educationists have condemned bookish knowledge. Gandhiji believed that school must be a 'doing things'. In basic system of education children acquire the knowledge of the formal school subjects as a by-product of purposeful activities.

IV. Social Activities and Community Life:

The corner-stone of Basic education lies in the activities and the community life of school. Apart from craft, productive activities and occupations find an important place in the curriculum of a basic school. Living together and doing together is the soul of any progressive system of education and basic system fully incorporates this in its curriculum and methods of teaching.

V. Self-Sufficiency:

Gandhiji felt that the educational system as introduced by the foreigners in India was expensive and it was very difficult for a poor country like India to spread education if it follows that system. So Gandhiji went a step further and declared that New Education must not only be worked centered but must also be self-supporting.

"...You have to start with the conviction that looking to the need of the villages of India our rural education ought to be made self-supporting if it is to be compulsory. This education ought to be for the kind of insurance against unemployment.

Not only from economic point of view, must this education be self-sufficient, but also from social and moral point of view. This means that at the end of the period of basic education the individual should become self-reliant and self-supporting."

VI. Modification of the Views of Mahatma Gandhi on Self-sufficiency

Dr. Zakir Hussain Committee pointed out the danger of overdoing of craft work and warned that oral work, drawing and expression work should not be lost sight of. The educative aspect is more important than the economic aspect. It thus shifted the emphasis from complete support to partial self-support. It was felt that with the earnings through sale of craft products, uniform for the students or mid-day meal or purchase of some necessary equipment may be made.

VII. Free and Compulsory Education:

Seven years free and compulsory education is one of the fundamentals of his scheme and this cardinal principle has been emphasized due to two reasons:

(i) India is a democratic country and success of democracy depends upon the enlightened citizens. Our great leaders like Gokhale worked for the introduction of compulsory education for long time. In his historic speech, Gokhale said that if elementary education was to spread in India, it must be made compulsory and if it was to be compulsory it must be free.

(ii) Gandhiji dream of classless society, free of exploitation — economic and social—can be realized only if everyone is educated

VIII. Mother Tongue as a Medium of Instruction:

It is now universally recognized that the young child can learn with great facility if the medium of instruction is its mother tongue. Gandhiji asserted that no education is possible through foreign medium and all elementary education must be imparted through the medium of mother tongue.

IX. Education through Correlation:

Correlation is one of the important feature and crux of basic education. In this scheme of education, Gandhiji wished to give knowledge as a compact whole. The modern educationist also advocated this. The basic education is therefore, an effort to correlate the life of the child with his immediate physical and social environment. It is an effort to make knowledge easier and at the same time more meaningful.

X. Integrated knowledge:

Basic education treats knowledge as an integrated whole. Curriculum is built around three integrally related centers:

(i) Physical environment,
(ii) Social environment, and
(iii) Craft work.

XI. Relationship with Life:

A basic school must become an active environment where teaching is not cut off from the life of the miniature community of the school and community itself. Education is to be directed to the need of life. It is not to pursue an idea which has no relation with or is totally isolated from the real situations of life.

XII. Training in Citizenship:

Basic education aims at developing ideas of mutual understanding and habits of cooperative and mutually helpful living among the students through its various practical and constructive programs the new education aims at giving the citizens of future a keen sense of personal warmth, dignity and efficiency. It is likely to strengthen in them the desire of self-improvement and social service in a cooperative community.

XIII. Greater freedom for the teacher and the taught:

In basic education, discipline does not mean order and external restraint but an intelligent use of freedom. The teacher gets many opportunities to make experiments, think for himself and put his idea and plan to practice.

XIV. The system was able to remove class and caste distinction.

It helps to bring social solidarity and national integration. It also removes the barriers between the educated and the non-educated, between manual work and intellectual work, between the rich and the poor and village and the town.

Basic education is not a class education: the ultimate objective of basic education is to create a social order in which there is no unnatural divisions between 'have' and 'have-nots' and everyone is assure of a living wage and the right to freedom.

XV. Basic education in rural as well as in urban areas:

It is wrong to assume that basic education is intended to be imparted in rural areas only. "In fact, in one sense there is greater need for basic education in urban areas than in rural areas. In rural areas the children who participate in the life of the farm or allied occupation of their families have certain types of further education. In performing their jobs the children come in to direct contact with actual life and with the experience they get forms the basis of further education. On the other hand in large towns and big industrial cities the children miss the opportunity for rich experiences and direct contact with life", observed Dr. K.L. Shrimali.

Limitations of Wardha Scheme

1. **Unsound Psychological Foundations of Wardha Scheme of Education:**

"The delicate but inexorable laws governing the development of the tender mind of the child have been completely ignored. The child is treated just as a policeman or a soldier, merely as a unit in a homogeneous mass. His individuality is ignored. He is viewed merely as a means to an end—the end being earning capacity and citizenship of sorts.

"Play is the only means by which creative energy can be released. Enlightened and informed educational opinion all over the civilized world is dedicatedly against forcing the child to learn a craft before he is twelve plus. It is nothing short of cruelty to make the child earn an anna or half an anna per hour during the stage when he ought to be playing and enjoying himself.

"There are three aspect of human nature—cognitive, affective and co native. The Wardha Scheme emphasizes the last aspect piously hoping that the student will wily-nilly get trained in the first through his training in the last. The middle aspect is completely ignored.

1.1 Undue Emphasis on Craft as the Only Basis of Correlation:

"It is impossible to establish any natural association between craft and all the subjects of cultural value which any sane system of education should cover through its curriculum. Teaching should be concrete and should be based on the child's active experience in his environment. But it is absurd to hang all knowledge from the peg of single craft.

1.2 No Place for Religious Education:

"Education suited to our national genius should have definite religious basis, with contempt of worldly pursuits in its core. Craft-centered education is decidedly alien to our ancient ideals.

2. **Basic Education not suited in an Age of Industrialization:**

As ours is a system of education which claims to produce an integrated individual, the emphasis is out of place in a community which has its face turned towards developing its economy to the full. So far Basic education fails to relate to the economic policy of state. But if this point is ignored, we shall find ourselves burdened with an educational system which turns out misfits even more rapidly than the one with which we are so dissatisfied .With rapid industrialization of India, knowledge of science and mathematics may become more desirable than skill in handicrafts.

2.1 Neglect of the child:

In a hurry to pay more attention to craft, it has neglected the child. Basic education is looked upon more as a social and economic duty than as a joyful adventure." A Craft is only a slogan, a fiction, which is practiced on commercial occasions for the benefits of visitors. In a basic school only two-third or half the normal time is given to academic education, the rest being taken up by crafts. And further, since on the time-table academic subjects generally come after the craft work, mostly agriculture, students are sometime too tired to take to academic work kindly .Students spend one-third or half the time for craft work without acquiring any dexterity worth speaking of in any craft.

CAUSES OF FAILURE OF BASIC EDUCATION

After the independence Basic scheme of education made good progress for about a decade but gradually due to several difficulties it failed to become a permanent and lasting feature of our educational system. The causes may be –

The self-supporting aspect of Basic Education received severe criticism in the academic circle. Teachers, social leaders and educational administrators had shown an indifferent attitude towards it. It was argued that the scheme turns a school into a centre of small scale industry. Moreover, teachers had to depend upon the earnings of the students. This had a demoralizing effect on teacher-pupil relationship.

Too much emphasis on craft had led the neglect of liberal education. Very often the craft is not properly selected from the point of view of education and social significance and teaching through craft had become just a slogan. Another criticism leveled against Basic Education was that a single craft can and should not be the basis of the entire educational process. It may not help in the development of liberal education and thus would create an imbalance in the educational system between vocational and intellectual education.

The method of correlation as technique of instruction was not stressed and sincerely followed. Correlation is no doubt a sound principle of education but correlation of the subjects through craft may appear to be sometimes unusual and time consuming.

Basic Education is often regarded as inferior type of education meant for the poor villagers. It has nothing to do with the urban people, who usually sent their children to modern type of schools. The general public had no confidence in basic schools because of the degraded social value accorded to it. Thus Basic education failed to become an integral part of our national system of education.

Basic Education can in no way help in the progress of modern scientific and technological development of the society, which was the need of the day. Rapid changes and modernization of our society can only be possible through the application of modern science and technology in the fields and factories.

Lack of finance and the absence of sound administrative policy were also responsible for the failure of Basic Education. Practically there was no coordination between the official and non-official agencies engaged in the organization and development of Basic education.

Teacher occupies the central position in Basic Education. Lack of adequate supply of efficient, trained and sincere teachers was one the most important cause for the failure of this scheme of education. Suitable orientation and training of teachers of basic schools was highly needed, which was rare. The majority of the teachers had no faith in this system.

Thus, it is quite justified to say that the fundamental principles of basic education are still valid and fruitful in the context of our present educational reform. They are relevant to be used as guiding principles of modern education. In fact, it needs to be reformed on modern lines then it may serve as one of the most interesting and fruitful techniques of instruction at elementary stage.

Gandhiji keenly wanted to create a new social order based on truth and non-violence. This can be brought about only through a silent social revolution. He believed that revolutionary change in the educational system can help to bring this silent social revolution. The scheme of Basic Education does not stand for mere technique, it stands for a new spirit and approach to all education

M. K. GANDHI'S VIEW TO RURAL RECONSTRUCTION

In the Indian context rural development may be defined as maximizing production in agriculture and allied activities in the rural areas including development of rural industries with emphasis on village and cottage industries.

It attaches importance to the generation of maximum possible employment opportunities in rural areas, especially for the weaker sections of the community so as to enable them to improve their standard of living.

Provision of certain basic amenities like drinking water, electricity, especially for the productive purpose, link roads connecting villages to market centers and facilities for health and education etc. figure prominently in the scheme of rural development.

Theoretically, Gandihian approach to rural development may be labeled as 'idealist'. It attaches supreme importance to moral values and gives primacy to moral values over material conditions. The Gandians believe that the source of moral values in general lies in religion and Hindu scriptures like the Upanishads and the Gita, in particular.

The concept of 'Rama Rajya' is the basis of Gandhis idea of an ideal social order. Gandhi defined Rama Rajya as "sovereignty of the people based on moral authority". He did not view Rama as a king, and people as his subjects. In the Gandihian scheme, 'Rama' stood for God or one's own 'inner voice' Gandhi believed in a democratic social order in which people are supreme. Their supremacy is, however, not absolute. It is subject to moral values.

Ideal Village:

The village is the basic unit of the Gandihian ideal social order. Gandhi succinctly pointed out, "If the village perishes India will perish too.... We have to make a choice between India of the villages that is as ancient as her and India of the cities which are a creation of foreign domination". Gandhi's ideal village belongs to the Pre-British period, when Indian villages were supposed to constitute the federation of selfgoverning autonomous republics.

According to Gandhiji, this federation will be brought about not by coercion or compulsion but by the voluntary offer of every village republic to join such a federation. The work of the central authority will only be to coordinate the work of different village republics and to supervise and manage things of common interest, as education, basic industries, health, currency, banking etc.

The central authority will have no power to enforce its decisions on village republics except the moral pressure or power of persuasion. The economic system and transport system introduced by the British have destroyed the "republican' character of the villages.

Gandhi, however, admitted that in olden times tyranny and oppression were in fact practiced by feudal chiefs. But, "odds were even". Today the odds are heavy. It is most demoralizing." In this way in the Gandihian scheme of things the ancient 'republic', an Indian village without tyranny and exploitation serves as a model unit.

Decentralisation:

Gandhi firmly believes that village republics can be built only through decentralization of social and political power. In such a system decision-making power will be vested in the Village Panchayat rather than in the State and the national capital. The representatives would be elected by all adults for a fixed period of five years. The elected representatives would constitute a council, called the Panchayat.

The Panchayat exercises legislative, executive and judicial functions. It would look after education, health and sanitation of the village. It would be the Panchayat responsibility to protect and uplift 'untouchables' and other poor people. Resources for Gandihian Approach to managing village affairs would be raised from the villages.

All the conflicts and disputes would be resolved within the village. And as far as possible not a single case is to be referred to courts outside the village. The Panchayat would play its role in propagating the importance of moral and spiritual values among the ruralites for bringing about rural reconstruction.

Apart from managing its own affairs the village would also be capable of defending itself against any invasion. A non-violent peace brigade of volunteers would be organized to defend the village. This corps would be different from the usual military formation. They would repose the utmost faith in non-violence and God.

Self-sufficiency:

Such a decentralized polity implies a decentralized economy. It can be attained only through self-sufficiency at the village level. The village should be self-sufficient as far as its basic needs – food, clothing, and other necessities – are concerned. The village has to import certain things which it cannot produce in the village. "We shall have to produce more of what we can, in order thereby to obtain in exchange, what we are unable to produce".

The village should produce food-crops and cotton in order to meet its requirements. Some lands should also be earmarked for cattle and for a playground for adults and children. If some land is still available, it should be used for growing useful cash crops like tobacco, opium, etc. to enable the village to get in exchange things which it does not produce.

Village economy should be planned with a view to providing full employment to all the adults of the village. Each man should be guaranteed employment to enable him to meet his basic needs in the village itself so that he is not forced to migrate to towns. In the ultimate analysis full employment should be linked with equality.

Physical labour occupies a central place in the Gandihian concept of the self-sufficient village. In this respect he was highly influenced by Rus-kin and Tolstoy. According to Gandhi, each man must do physical labour to earn his bread. Physical labour is necessary for moral discipline and for the sound development of the mind. Intellectual labour is only for one's own satisfaction and one should not demand payment for it.

The needs of the body must be supplied by the body. Gandhi said, "If all labored for their bread then there would be enough food and enough leisure for all." Shriman Narayan rightly observes, "Gandhiji recognized toil to be not a curse but the joyful business of life as it has the power to make man healthier, merrier, fitter and kindlier".

Industrialization:

Gandhiji maintained that industrialization would help only a few and will lead to concentration of economic power. Industrialization leads to passive or active exploitation of the villages. It encourages competition. Large scale production requires marketing. Marketing means profit-seeking through an exploitative mechanism.

Moreover, industrialization replaces manpower and hence it adds to unemployment. In a country like India, where millions of labourers in the villages do not get work for even six months in a year, industrialization will not only increase unemployment but force labourers to migrate to urban areas. This will ruin villages.

In order to avoid such a catastrophe, village and cottage industries should be revived. They provide employment to meet the needs of the villagers and facilitate village self-sufficiency. Gandians are not against machine per se if it meets two aims: self-sufficiency and full employment. According to Gandhi, there would be no objection to villagers using even the modern machines and tools that they could make and could afford to use. Only they should not be used as a means of exploitation of others.

Trusteeship:

Gandhiji was not against the institution of private property. But he wanted to restrict the right of private property to what was necessary to yield an honourable livelihood. For the excess he prescribed the principle of trusteeship.

Gandhiji emphasized the principle of trusteeship in social and economic affairs. He firmly believed that all social property should be held in trust. The capitalists would take care not only of themselves but also of others. Some of their surplus wealth would be used for the rest of the society.

The poor workers, under trusteeship, would consider the capitalists as their benefactors; and would repose faith in their noble intentions. Gandhiji felt that if such a trusteeship were established, the welfare of the workers would increase and the clash between the workers and employers would be avoided. Trusteeship would help considerably "in realising a state of equality on earth."

Gandhiji firmly believed that land should not be owned by any individual. Land belongs to God. Hence, individual ownership of land should be shunned. For that a landowner should be persuaded to become a trustee of his land. He should be convinced that the land he owns does not belong to him. Land belongs to the community and must be used for the welfare of the community. They are merely trustees. By persuasion the heart of landowners should be changed and they should be induced to donate their land voluntarily.

If the land owners do not oblige and continue to exploit the poor workers, the latter should organize non-violent, non- cooperation, civil disobedience struggles against them. Gandhiji rightly held the view that "no person can amass wealth without the cooperation, willing or forced, of the people concerned".

If this knowledge were to penetrate and spread amongst the poor, they would become strong and learn how to free themselves from the crushing inequalities which have pushed them to the verge of starvation. But the oppressed should not take recourse to violent methods. In the Gandihian scheme of things, the principle of cooperation, love and service is most important and violence has no place in it. Violence is against "moral values' and civilized society is inconceivable in the absence of moral values.

Gandhis concept of development is oriented to the uplift of the common man. He preferred village habitats to megalopolises and Swadeshi craft to imported technology for the economic wellbeing of the common man. He stressed the need for cottage industries in place of gigantic industries and advocated for a decentralized economy instead of a centralized one.

He realized the need for integrated rural development and believed that education, health and vocation should be properly integrated. He emphasized the need for education and training which he called 'Naitalim' (New training) for rural reconstruction.

In fine, Gandihian approach to rural development strives to reconstruct village republics which would be non-violent, self- governed and self-sufficient so far as the basic necessities of ruralites are concerned. Apart from creating a new socio-economic order, it Endeavour's to transform man; otherwise the changes in the socio-economic order will be short-lived.

Chapter 05
Appropriateness of Gandhian educational thought in 21stcentury with special reference to NEP 2020

New education for rebuilding moral India

Education must come through ordinary business of life. The teaching methods for the adult and child would generally be different. Audio method is suitable method for adults, while stories prayers, lives of saints are good for children. Children should not have to go through long-hours of teaching. Learning with the rest, and learning with excursion, learning by doing, learning by going nearer to the nature and society. Some important aspect of learning which cannot be taught osrally should be taught through direct contact and experiencing learning through "eye on" and "hand on" experience.

New system of education would reconsider conceptualizations of teaching, learning and researching. Education encompassing a concern; or human rights; a culture of peace. Education is a fundamental element in all processes that aim to build a culture of peace, human rights. This involves something more than the provisions of information; it is a lifelong value-based process of improving knowledge and action within the framework of principles of truth, non-violence, Satyagraha. In the context of deep human crises in the 21st century, the education of future citizens heads to be redressed between academics and human rights.

The single minded focus on economic growth and globalization over much of 20th and 21st century has led to an erosion of human values. The making of moral citizens must mean persons with human excellence which includes strength of character, inner resources, and family society and so on.

Connected to the question of excellence is the issue of ranking of Indian universities in relation to universities in various countries. Certain organizations in the world have come up with the statistics that not Indian university is in the list of top 200 which are assessed to be excellent and sought after by the foreigners. It is felt by many that this is a matter of worry for India. It may be noted that certain other assessments have argued that Indian education is far superior to education in other countries.

These issues cannot be tackled merely by changing educational formula such as 2+3+2. While planning for the educational system in the future, the wise policy would be to shun global competition. The Swadeshi and Swaraj are the best concepts over which a world-class educational system can be built.

The best minds in the world, viz. Russell, Hayek, Gandhi, Vinoba, and Vivekananda have been perturbed or worried in the 20th Century. The vast numbers of people have been suffering from despair, loneliness, bewilderment, cynicism, and so on. This has been so in spite of ample, achieved know how.

Education plays a very important part in the birth, growth, and death of civilizations. Such is the importance of education in human life. Present human civilization is in crises because today's education is in crises. But the educational crises cannot be tackled; the problems of education cannot be solved by mere organization, administration, or money. The education is breaking down not so much because of, say, over-specification but because of the absence of metaphysical awareness. We are suffering from a metaphysical disease, and the cure, therefore, must be metaphysical. Education which fails to clarify our central concerns is mere training or indulgence. For it is our central concerns that are in disorder, and, and as long as the present anti-metaphysical temper persists, the disorder will grow worse. Education, for from ranking as men's greatest resource, will then be an agent of destruction (Schumacher, 1965, pp. 70-92).

A. Huxley has argued that there are three main categories of defects-sacrifice of the individual to the system, psychologically unsound methods of teaching, and irrational methods of imposing discipline. We need a new system of universal education of the same kind as that which has proved it. We need a system of individual education (Selected Essays, 1972, p.60).

Gandhi have contributed a new galaxy of altogether original ideas, Terms, concepts, programmes, viz. Swadeshi, Swaraj, Nai Talim, Satyagraha, and Constructive works programme (CWP). This programme is intimately connected with the revolution of education. It was meant to promote both basic education and the adult education. The primary aim of CWP was the elimination of illiteracy in India. In order to achieve this, Gandhi advocated that women also should be provided liberal education. And in order to ensure that this should happen actually, he recommended that women should be provided scholarships. CWP occupies unique importance in

Gandiana, i.e., Gandian evolutionary and revolutionary mass-oriented, pratical, wellbeing enhancing programming and other activities. His thinking on these programmes has influenced his philosophy of education.

Gandhiji restructured the curriculum such that manual labour and literary studies in a balanced manner which will release immense creative energies. The teaching of handcrafts as the pivot or centre of the whole educational programmed would involve reforms/revolution. The ultimate purpose of education would then be progress in rural areas or villages. "My plan is also to impart primary education through the medium of village handicrafts is thus conceived as the spearhead of silent social revolution fraught with the most far-reaching consequences. It will provide a healthy and moral basis of relationship between the city and village." (Glyn, p.30)

RELEVANCE OF GANDHIS EDUCATIONAL THOUGHT IN PRESENT SOCIAL CONTEXT

Gandhiji has given a scientific argument for the education system. He says the goal of education is the development of spiritual character strength. Education is the body's response to the mind. Even today, education psychologists have identified the teacher as a means of overall development of the individual. He spoke of teaching through that mother tongue. He spoke of the harmony between the school and the home environment and of making education unpaid. All of this is currently in effect. However, in some cases, due to the negligence of the government or for social reasons, these features of the education system are not being fulfilled. Because the children of a poor family are leaving school in search of food and are being employed in various jobs. But now the government is trying to bring all children under school through universal education which was once wanted by Gandhiji. But the heartfelt teachings that Gandhiji spoke of are always being tried. So that everyone gets a chance to develop their own personality.

He did not give precedence to biblical knowledge as an instrument of education. According to him, teachers will be instrumental in writing textbooks for children. Attempts have been made to give more prominence to the present education. He argues that productive work should be an important part of education planning. Without the medium of subject-based learning, students will not soon forget what they will learn in a practical way. He spoke about the important role of teachers in this regard, but at present in the field of education and teachers are teaching with a business-minded attitude, as a result, the work of teachers in the institution has become a kind of charity work.

The entrepreneurial spirit of private educational institutions can be nurtured. Gandhiji said that if a child has to go to school in the primary stage, then it should be seen that the school should be like his home and the teachers should be like his parents. Schools are taught in a culture-friendly home environment. In this case, at present, some states have a definite need for it, but the state spends its money.

At present, both the state government and the Center are spending money on education so that they can come under education in the morning. If the government takes different programs, it takes time to implement those programs due to lack of proper mentality of different departments or many times those works are not being implemented. On the other hand, all the things she said about women's education, adult education and religious education are being followed very well now and then. There has been an unimaginable improvement in women's education. Evidence of women's participation in women's education and employment. The government has also passed a new bill for women. Night schools have been set up in the interest of improving adult education. Various actions are being taken by the government to curb the spread of religion at all levels of the society.

PRESENT RELEVANCE OF GANDHIS BASIC EDUCATION:

According to Gandhiji, holistic development of the child is one of the goals of basic education. This education makes the child socially oriented. This goal of education is currently being pursued. The way the education system has been developed for all-round development. The goal of Gandhis basic education was education through action. Teaching a child by reading a book will not be able to comprehend the content and will soon be forgotten as a punishment to the child. At present, arrangements have been made for teaching. The views of education psychologists are justified after fulfilling the responsibilities, the average oil. Of this education system this education has now penetrated into their homes through the elderly men or women who come under this education.

After independence, however, there were no aforementioned obstacles to the progress of basic education. We have adopted democratic communism as the national ideology after independence. With this ideology, Gandhis basic education plan is not short. The national government therefore suggested that the basic education plan be fully implemented in different states. Various advisory committees were formed to make basic education up-to-date; The National Institute of Basic Education was established. But reviewing the real situation, it can be seen that this education policy has completely failed. Dr. Zakir Hassan who put Gandhis education policy into practice through the Wardha Plant the reason for this failure. A lot can be found by searching. As the search for those reasons progresses, two aspects can be summarized.

A class of people in the society is enjoying special opportunities sssas a result, in the minds of ordinary people. Aversion to this basic education was transmitted. That is, our lack of a proper social and state vision has pushed basic education to fruition. In addition, some of the basic organizational shortcomings of basic education and the lack of suitable teachers for management have led to its failure. However, this education policy is absolutely necessary for the reform of the national education system. This has been acknowledged in the report of the Education Commission of India. So in the latest effort to restructure the education system in India, the concept of action-oriented education in basic education has been adopted in a slightly changed form. Unemployment is on the rise at the current rate at which the world's population has grown.

Gandhis basic education is needed to overcome this unemployment. Because students or unemployed youths, young women will earn their education expenses with the help of their own handicrafts and their own labor and will get some relief from unemployment. This form of loan is being given by the government to encourage small scale cottage industries. Unemployment seems to be declining a bit through this and this is where Gandhis basic education is successful. A commission was formed in 1944 under the chairmanship of John Sergeant to make the basic education system a success. In 1955, the central government reconstituted a committee, and in 1984, the Kothari Committee focused on basic education. Many colleges were built for this. NSS plans have been put in place in colleges and universities to make basic education a success.

NATIONAL EDUCATIONAL POLICY 2020 AND GANDHI EDUCATIONAL THOUGHT

The world is passing through an age of critical thinking, rational analysis and scientific temper. Hence, the focus in the new learning is not only to gain knowledge or learn, but more so on how to learn. In line with this demand NEP 2020 document proposes to develop a human resource pool who can think critically. The focus in NEP 2020 is on how to learn which is the primary condition for development of scientific temper enshrined in the directive principle of the Indian constitution. This idea of learning being promoted by NEP 2020 finds echo in Gandhian thought, conceived during British period, too for whom education was incomplete without the element of learning. According to Mahatma Gandhi the education should be able to fulfill and satisfy the needs of the three components essential for enlightenment of the human being viz. the body, the mind and the spirit. However, the education system in vogue during the British period gave primacy to mind and intelligence and ignored the body and the spirit. NEP 2020 echoes the same tone and philosophy as that Mahatma Gandhis thought of learning for the body, the mind and the spirit. Its overtones are reflected in NEP 2020 where in it suggests a series of curricular and pedagogy reforms to implement the idea of learning how to learn, cleanliness, hygiene, community service and character development.

Gandhi believed that the education was meant for life, education had the purpose to serve through life and throughout life. Gandhi believed in the balance among skill development, community service, cleanliness, spiritual enrichment and education. NEP 2020 also talks about hygiene and cleanliness, ethics and spiritual enrichment, cooperation and community service so as to keep students connected to the humanity and environment, and to the society. Thus we find the reverberations of Gandhi's vision of education spelt out in British period in NEP 2020.

Gandhi believed in the system of education that would make the learner self-reliant. Gandhi believed that the education should make youth employable in addition to making the youth better human being. Hence, skill development and vocational training should be part of the curriculum. This would make the learner capable of leading life independently. The prevalent education system was making students only imitators, (as it was required during the British period). He wanted students to have the questioning ability who could engage in meaningful dialogue and discussion with their mentors. The education system should create active learning environment in which students could develop critical and rational thinking. Incidentally, NEP 2020 has spelt out the need for creating educational environment where in the learner should become not imitators but creators of the new knowledge.

Glossary

1. Ashram: A place where a group of Hindus live together away from the rest of society, or a place where Hindus can go in order to pray.
2. Aparigraha: Nonpossession
3. Atman: The spiritual life principle of the universe, especially when regarded as immanent in the individual's real life.
4. Ahimsa: Non violence
5. Artha: Sense, goal, purpose or essence.
6. Ahimsa: (In the Hindu, Buddhist, & Jainism tradition) respect for all living things and avoidance of violence towards others.
7. Bapu: The father of Nation.
8. Bhagavad Gita: The Holy book of Hindus.
9. Brahmacharya: Celibacy
10. Buniyaadi Shiksha: Basic Education
11. Charkha: Spinning Wheel
12. Dhoti: Loose trousers
13. Dharma: In Hinduism, dharma is the religious and moral law governing individual conduct and is one of the four ends of life.
14. Darshanam: Vision
15. Ektara: One-string
16. Grihastashram: Homestead/ Householder.
17. Gurukula: The word gurukula is a combination of the Sanskrit words Guru ('Teacher' or 'Master') and Kula ('Family' or 'Home'), the term is

also used today to refer to residential monasteries or schools operated by modern gurus.

18. Guru – Shishya: Teacher- disciple relation.
19. Guru: A spiritual teacher/ leader.
20. Harijan: A member of the outcaste group in India: untouchable.
21. Hartal: A closure of shops and offices as a protest or a mark of sorrow/ strike.
22. Iliad: A series of miseries or disastrous events.
23. Jeevan: Life
24. Jhanji: A broken or perforated coin, a cowry or shall with a broken top.
25. Karmayoga: A path to reach moksha (spiritual liberation) through work.
26. Laay: Honour, bashfulness
27. Maharshi: Religious sage, a teacher of spiritual and mystical knowledge.
28. Mahapurush: Affectionate great man.
29. Moksha: Salvation
30. Mantra: Especially in Hinduism and Buddhism a word or sound that is believed to have a special spiritual power.
31. Mukhti: Liberation.
32. Moksha: Liberation
33. Nirala Mahapurush: Exceptionally great man.
34. Nanga Fakir: Naked Saint
35. Nai: New
36. Nai-Talim: New Education
37. Purdah: The practice in certain Muslim and Hindu societies of screening women from man or strangers, especially to observe Purdah.
38. Ramanama: The name of Lord God
39. Ram Rajya: Ram Rajya is a system where the society is run by principles of Lord Rama.

40. Samabhava: Equitability
41. Satyagraha: A policy of passive political resistance, especially that advocated by Mahatma Gandhi against British rule in India.
42. Swaraj: Self-Rule
43. Sanyasashram: Heritage
44. Sanskrit: Ancient language which used to be spoken in India.
45. Samavaya: Coming together, contact, congress, crowd
46. Talim: Education
47. Takli: Spindle
48. Vedic: The language used in the Vedas, an early form of Sanskrit.

Bibliography

BOOKS

- Agarwal, L.B.: The Harijans in Rebellion, Taraporewala, Bombay, 1934
- Agarwal, J.C. and Gupta S.: *Great Philosophers and Thinkers on Education*, Shipra Publications, Delhi, 2014.
- Ahir, D.C.: Gandhi and Ambedkar: A comparative Study, Blumoon, New Delhi, 1995.
- Alter, Joseph S.: Gandhi's Body: Sex, Diet, and the politics of Nationalism, University of Pennsylvania press, Philadelphia, 2000.
- Ambedkar, B.R.: Mr. Ghandi and the Emancipation of the untouchables, Thacker & Co., Bombay, 1943
- Anand, J. H.: Dalit Literature is the Literature of protest, Dalit solidarity, Delhi, 1995.
- Atal, Yogesh: The changing frontiers of caste, National Publishing House, Delhi, 1968.
- Bakshi, S.R.: *Gandhi and Champaran Satyagraha*, Akashdeep Pub. House, Delhi, 1988
- Bandyopadhyaya, *Jayantanuja: Social and Political thought of Gandhi*, Allied Publishers, Bombay, 1969.
- Bari, S.A.: *Gandhi's Doctrine of Civil Resistance*, Kalamkar Prakashan, New Delhi, 1971.
- Bharti, Brahm Datt: *Gandhi and Gandhism Unmasked: Was Gandhi a Traitor?* India: Erabooks, New Delhi. 1992
- Bhatt, V.: *The Harijans of Maharashtra*, All Indian Harijan Sevak Sangh, Delhi, 1941.
- Bondurant, Joan: Conquest of Violence: *The Gandhian Philosophy of Conflict*, University of California Press, Berkeley, 1971.

- Broman, William: *Gandhi and Non-violence,* State University of New York Press, New York, 1986.
- Bhole, L.M.: *Educational Philosophy of Mahatma Gandhi and Vinoba Bhave,* Shipra Publications, New Delhi, 2017.
- Cohn, Bernard S.: *The Changing Status of a Depressed Caste,* the University of Chicago Press, Chicago, 1955.
- Joshi, Sudharma .: *Educational Thoughts Of Mahatma Gandhi,* Crescent Publications, Delhi, 2008
- Mukalel, C. Joseph.: *Gandian Education,* Discovery Publishing House, Delhi, 1997.
- Pruthi, R.K. & Chaturvedi Archna, *Gandhian Education,* Commonwealth Publications, New Delhi, 2009
- Pathak, Ramesh Prasad & Bhardwaj, Amita Panday.: *The Educational Thinkers of East and West,* Kanishka Publications, New Delhi, 2017
- Tripathi, Sridhar.: *Gandhi's Philosophy Of Education,* Anmol Publications, New Delhi, 2007

ONLINE SOURCES (NEWS PAPERS, LETTERS AND REPORTS)

- Harijan, 31 July 1937
- Harijan, 02 October 1937
- Harijan, 25 August 1946
- Harijan, 09 November 1947
- Indian opinion, 19 August 1911
- Letter to Narahari Parikh, 17 May 1917
- Letter to Aanandibai, 22 August 1927
- Letter to Tarabehn Modak, 16 October.1945
- Navajivan, 17 August 1925
- Navajivan, 20 May 1928
- Navajivan, 02 June 1929
- Young India, 06 August 1925
- Report of the Education Commission (1964-66), sections 01.27-01.29
- Report of the Review committee on " The Curriculum for the ten-year school" (1977), chapter 03, PP. 10-11